Closing the Circle

*Pursah's Gospel of Thomas
and A Course in Miracles*

First published by O Books, 2008
O Books is an imprint of John Hunt Publishing Ltd., The Bothy, Deershot Lodge, Park Lane, Ropley,
Hants, SO24 0BE, UK
office1@o-books.net
www.o-books.net

Distribution in:

UK and Europe
Orca Book Services
orders@orcabookservices.co.uk
Tel: 01202 665432 Fax: 01202 666219
Int. code (44)

USA and Canada
NBN
custserv@nbnbooks.com
Tel: 1 800 462 6420 Fax: 1 800 338 4550

Australia and New Zealand
Brumby Books
sales@brumbybooks.com.au
Tel: 61 3 9761 5535 Fax: 61 3 9761 7095

Far East (offices in Singapore, Thailand,
Hong Kong, Taiwan)
Pansing Distribution Pte Ltd
kemal@pansing.com
Tel: 65 6319 9939 Fax: 65 6462 5761

South Africa
Alternative Books
altbook@peterhyde.co.za
Tel: 021 555 4027 Fax: 021 447 1430

Text copyright Rogier Fentener van Vlissingen
2008

Design: Stuart Davies

ISBN: 978 1 84694 113 9

A CIP catalogue record for this book is available
from the British Library.

Permissions:
Portions of A Course in Miracles © 1975, 1985, 1992, used by permission of the Foundation for
A Course in Miracles.
Portions of The Disappearance of the Universe © 2003 and Your Immortal Reality © 2006,
by Gary R. Renard, used by permission of the author.
All other material quoted from other sources herein is reproduced by virtue of the Fair Use
provisions of the U.S. Copyright Law.

Cover art, the painting "Teach Only Love" by Samuel Augustin, © 2007
NYCW/TheCourseInTongues, reproduced by permission from The Course In Tongues, a Chapter of
New York Citiworks.

Printed by Chris Fowler International

O Books operates a distinctive and ethical publishing philosophy in
all areas of its business, from its global network of authors to
production and worldwide distribution.
This book is produced on FSC certified stock, within ISO14001
standards. The printer plants sufficient trees each year through
the Woodland Trust to absorb the level of emitted carbon in
its production.

Closing the Circle

*Pursah's Gospel of Thomas
and A Course in Miracles*

Rogier Fentener van Vlissingen

BOOKS

Winchester, UK
Washington, USA

"Those who found solace in *A Course in Miracles* and recent books of Gary Renard will most certainly be intrigued by this work. In *Closing the Circle*, Rogier van Vlissingen takes us on a scholarly, yet uniquely personal journey through the Logia of awakening. This book clearly reveals a unique ability to tease apart the wonderful teachings of Jesus in such a way that lends to absorption in the word."

Mick Quinn, author of *Power and Grace: The Wisdom of Awakening*.

Contents

Foreword

by Gary R. Renard

I first met Rogier van Vlissingen in New York City in November of 2003. At that time, I had barely begun speaking in public about the experiences that were chronicled in my first book, *The Disappearance of the Universe* (now sometimes referred to by its readers as "DU"). The book had been published just eight months earlier, and I had refused to speak in public the first six months that it was available to the public. The reason for that was simple. I did not want to because I was scared to death of the idea of speaking in front of people. It would take two more years for me to learn to forgive *that*.

When I met Rogier, I found him to be unusually interesting in his brief but blunt observations about Jesus (not his real name) and the origins of the statements that, rightly or wrongly, were attributed to that master by the historical figures who shared the stage with him two thousand years ago.

For that reason, I was not completely surprised when Rogier went on to share some of his brilliant observations at an on-line discussion group that was set up to publicly discuss the teachings of DU. Rogier had an obvious ability to state certain ideas, a couple of which I am citing here, because they led me to the realization that this was a man who had something important to say.

Rogier was very articulate in expressing that *The Disappearance of the Universe* was the bridge between the Gospel of Thomas, that first and most fascinating of the Gospels, and *A Course in Miracles*, which is a modern but timeless spiritual masterpiece that clearly has the Voice of Jesus as its Teacher.

I should point out that when I call the Gospel of Thomas a "Gospel," even the "Jesus Seminar," a group of distinguished biblical scholars, included Thomas as one of the five Gospels to be

1

taken seriously. I personally would not limit the number to five, but I think it is interesting that the Jesus Seminar included Thomas in the book *The Five Gospels.*

The more I read Rogier's work, the more I realized that it was not idle theory but intricate details of scholarship that had led to his observations. For example, he points out that certain Christian terms in their original Greek form meant something different from what they mean in English today. For example, the word "repent" in Greek originally meant "change of mind"; today, the word "repent" is about changing your behavior and cleaning up your act on the level of form.

It is not just that Christianity got Jesus wrong, it even got Christianity wrong. Then, going back to the beginning and as Rogier explains within these pages, it was the theology of the Apostle Paul—*not* the teachings of Jesus—that became the basis of Christianity. Although that may be a very provocative position to some, there is a growing propensity of evidence that seems destined to make this the majority viewpoint within decades, which, in the overall scheme of things, would be remarkably fast.

If, like me, you are fascinated with the subject of how a pure message of love and forgiveness could be convoluted into one of suffering and sacrifice, yet would somehow resurface and eventually thrive, simply because it is impossible to bury the truth forever, then this is the book for you.

I sincerely believe that anyone with an open mind will find *Closing the Circle* to be not just entertaining reading, but an exposé of how a great message got lost and how it is being regained.

Gary R. Renard

Preface

In the months after the publication of Gary Renard's *The Disappearance of the Universe* (DU), I found myself making contributions to the on-line group on Yahoo! which discusses the book, commenting on how a revisionist history of Early Christianity, based on the notion that Thomas predates Paul, ties in with *The Disappearance of the Universe*, and I was surprised and delighted when some time later Gary asked me for permission to include one of my postings on that forum in his upcoming book. Little did I know that he was going to use it as the very introduction to Pursah's version of the Gospel of Thomas (P/GoTh) in his second book, *Your Immortal Reality* (YIR), which appeared in 2006. I can only say that it was a very profound experience for me when I finally did see it in print, and it confirmed for me a vague feeling of being somehow connected to the developments during the period of Gary's writing of the book.

It took all of *A Course in Miracles* (abbr. ACIM, or "the Course"), *The Disappearance of the Universe*, and *Your Immortal Reality*, not to mention the Thomas Gospel itself, for me to arrive at this point. Yet, the opportunity more or less presented itself to me on a silver platter and seemed like the logical outflow of my participation in that on-line forum about *The Disappearance of the Universe*, which is affectionately known as "the DU-group" on Yahoo.com. A bit later, I started a thread in that group for a discussion of the seventy Logia of Pursah's kernel of the Gospel of Thomas as they now appear in their entirety in Chapter 7 of *Your Immortal Reality* (pp. 162 ff.), whereupon some participants recommended very early on that this material ought to become a book. After a moment of surprise, I realized that a book would be a natural development culminating from the discussions and would be a great project to work on. And so, here it is.

A quick exchange of emails with Gary Renard, who is, after all, the proximate cause of all this trouble, since he authored both *The Disappearance of the Universe* and *Your Immortal Reality*, assured me of his support and guidance. In a September 7, 2006, email message to me, he wrote: "As for Thomas, if you feel guided to do it, I'd like YIR to be used and credited for the sayings and the 22 explanations that appear in DU to be considered for meaning." Those directions made complete sense to me.

At an earlier time, when Gary first disclosed in the DU-group that Arten and Pursah were back (see the section "Closing the Circle—Notes on Pursah's Gospel of Thomas") and there would be a second book, I had a very profound intuition that I somehow knew the gist of the second book, almost to the point where I felt I was part of the process, though I could not have put it into words. The essence of my feeling at that time was that the connection of *A Course in Miracles* to the Thomas sayings would be much expanded and elaborated upon in the new book. What had been clear to me was that *The Disappearance of the Universe*, besides never compromising the Course even one iota, even while explaining it in everyday language, or "vernacular," as Gary likes to call it with a twenty-five cent word, extended *A Course in Miracles* with a positive identification of the Thomas sayings as originating from the same Jesus as the Jesus of the Course.

*

One obvious challenge concerning Thomas stems from the fact that, as we now know, some of the sayings were corrupted as they were passed along and others added on after the fact. Filtering out such corruptions should be easy, for some are intuitively obvious, but it never is, unless you have textual sources that show variations. Enter Pursah, whose steady-hand rendering of the text produced a new "kernel" of the Thomas gospel, the authenticity of which she vouches for. The decision to trust Pursah as a reliable source in this regard is evidently a personal one, but what can be said with certainty is that many of her edits make immediate and obvious intuitive sense. The logical basis of the current approach is explained in the Introduction, and some further details are explained in the "Closing the Circle—Authenticity and Corruption" section, while in Index 3 there is a comparison for all of the Logia with a more traditional text-critical approach.

In *A Course in Miracles,* Jesus alludes to inaccuracies in the biblical tradition itself in some places, as well as misinterpretation of it in other places, and at various levels offers corrections or clarifications to the Christian understanding of his message. But with the positive identification of the inner consistency of the Thomas sayings with *A Course in Miracles,* a more explicit and positive connection is laid between a pre-Pauline Jesus, as we hear him in the Thomas tradition, and the Jesus of the Course. And this profound consistency and continuity of thought forges the link between the elaborate and highly sophisticated non-dualism of *A Course in Miracles* and the Gospel of Thomas.

For the rest, the wonderful environment of the DU-group on Yahoo! provided the soil for this project to take root and start to grow. This type of process seemed ideal to me for the development of a book such as this one, comparable to teaching a course at a university, which provides a perfect laboratory for the creation of a book; in such a situation, ideas can be refined over time and made ready for formal publication. Likewise, I have been discussing the sayings in my own Course workshops in New York City. So herewith, thanks goes to all members of the DU-group, as well as my own study group, for their participation and encouragement; to Gary Renard for his enthusiastic support; and to all my many teachers of *A Course in Miracles,* most specifically Kenneth Wapnick, Ph.D., and my dear friend Jeffrey M. Seibert, Ph.D.

It may also be worthwhile recording here, as has been highlighted elsewhere by Gary Renard, that *The Disappearance of the Universe* appeared simultaneously with Elaine Pagels' *Beyond*

Belief and Dan Brown's *The Da Vinci Code*. Somehow, those three books roused interest in the Thomas gospel and other extra-canonical literature to new levels. Pagels' book is a serious conversation with the reader, and she comes at the subject from a standpoint of her own attraction to, but ambivalent relationship with, the Christian tradition, as well as her interest in exploring beyond its boundaries. It clearly hit a nerve with the readership, and as a result it greatly stimulated curiosity about the Thomas material. *The Da Vinci Code* is an enjoyable and fanciful novel that conjures up wild possibilities and derives its excitement mostly from a juvenile anti-authoritarian sentiment that the Church has held back, suppressed, and destroyed information. While this is historically accurate on one level, it is possible to overdo such a viewpoint, for even if the Church may have suppressed and eradicated a lot that is true, conversely it is not an *a priori* given that all that was thus lost is by definition worth keeping, which seems to be the tendentious implication of books like *The Da Vinci Code*.

In this context, we should simply note that Gary Renard's work, which relies on *A Course In Miracles* as the source for understanding the teachings of Jesus (or "J," as he calls him), provides a refreshing and different angle to the problem. In effect, once you see the connection between the Jesus of the Thomas sayings and the Jesus of *A Course In Miracles*, a very coherent view of the Thomas gospel does emerge. On the other hand, if the Jesus of *A Course In Miracles* makes no sense to you, that connection will not mean much. This book aims to document some of the underlying logic of the connection, without necessarily requiring an in-depth knowledge of *A Course In Miracles* at first. However, for the reader who finds this book first, if what is presented here makes any sense at all, so will *A Course In Miracles*, as well as Gary Renard's books.

Lastly, a comment on the various editions of the Thomas gospel is in order. Through working with the text of Pursah's version, I have found that there really is little merit in comparing her version with the Nag Hammadi text, for henceforth we are concerned merely with the content of the material, if we accept Pursah's version. For a long time, I had planned to include in this book the text of one acceptable Thomas translation from the Coptic manuscript from the Nag Hammadi collection, but I had trouble coming to terms with it on account of the dual challenges of choosing the right version of the text and obtaining the necessary permissions to quote the material. Meanwhile I noticed in discussions in my workshops that the historical text quickly became irrelevant to most people. Besides, there are so many Thomas translations—and I realize that most readers probably have their own preference for one—that, in the end, I decided to keep the discussion of the differences between P/GoTh and the Nag Hammadi-based versions (historically the only complete source) strictly generic and not specific to any particular edition.

After looking at the situation even cursorily, we can simply leave the vagaries and uncertainties of the historical text behind. The differences between P/GoTh and the translations of the historical text are discussed in a generic sense for each of the sayings. Having said that, the reader could use any available Thomas text he chooses for comparison. If you are looking for one, the first choice must be Marvin Meyer's, since Pursah recommended it once to Gary Renard in a non-published commentary (this was at a time before her own version of the Thomas kernel was published in *Your Immortal Reality*), and he in turn has shared that recommendation on the DU-group. The second choice may be the Scholars Version, on account of the fact that, on a few occasions, Pursah uses some word choices that are fairly similar to those found in the corresponding sections of that translation. See the Bibliography for details. Note also that I am maintaining a blog on materials related to this book, including discussions of the Thomas editions I have consulted and other materials. It is at www.xanga.com/rogierfvv.

Thanks goes out to all the people who contributed to this book with their feedback, including Lucia Espinosa and several others. Christine de Lignières was the incomparable editor, whose contribution was invaluable in helping me to bring out what I wanted to say from what I wrote whenever I became blind to my own verbiage. As to proofreading, I must thank the incomparable Lenore Dittmar. I could not have done it without her, and "picayune details" gained new meaning—for one thing, false modesty on her part—as the ability to notice these seems to be a rare skill. My thanks goes out to the Foundation for *A Course in Miracles* for the permission to quote from the Course and to Gary Renard for his permission to use the material from his books. Last but not least, I want to recognize Linda Jackson-Kemp, who, indirectly in many ways, is almost the godmother of this book by virtue of her undying support in assuring me of a quiet spot amidst the noises of city life to enable the writing of this book. I ask forgiveness from anyone I failed to mention, as there were many others supporting me in one way or another. Without a lot of support, the completion of any book like this one is impossible. Any mistakes that remain are strictly mine.

Introduction

GARY: Makes sense to me.

PURSAH: He's right on the money, bro.

And that actually makes a good introduction to

a little surprise I have for you.[1]

At the outset of this book, we might perhaps paraphrase *A Course in Miracles* (ACIM, in the Epilogue of the Workbook) in saying that this book is a beginning, not an end. Pursah is very clear in *Your Immortal Reality* when she says:

> Nevertheless, no matter what scripture they're reading, people should eventually become their own ministers and interpreters, using the Holy Spirit as their guide. That's actually part of the process of returning to, or re-becoming Spirit, which is what they really are. (YIR, p. 160).

And so the focus of this book is an exploration of—and perhaps the start of a dialogue amongst students on—these early teachings of Jesus. As such, one might hope it would serve as a path of discovery in our own individual relationship with our Internal Teacher. In that spirit, the book grew out of a series of postings in the Yahoo! group which deals with *The Disappearance of the Universe*, also known as the DU-group.

I should add that only during my work on this project have I come to realize how few people are at all familiar with the

---

1 *Your Immortal Reality* (see Bibliography), p. 159. The quote refers to the material I contributed to the Yahoo! group on *The Disappearance of the Universe* (during the time *Your Immortal Reality* was being written), and which was subsequently used as an introduction to Pursah's version of the Thomas gospel in that book (pp. 157 ff.). This introduction is, in effect, an expanded and corrected version of my comments in the Yahoo! group. An amended version of the original posting can be found in Appendix 1.

Thomas gospel, while in my own experience it has been around almost all of my life, beginning in ca. 1960 (I was about nine years old), when my parents attended a lecture by Prof. Gilles Quispel, who was one of the first translators of the complete Thomas gospel from the Coptic. There was an excitement in the air, then, about finally getting actual words of Jesus as opposed to the colorized version of Paul and friends, which was called Christianity. Most unfortunately, the impact the Thomas gospel might have had ended up being blunted by a tendency to suspect that the Thomas material was not much older than the oldest document, which originates from the second century of the Common Era (Oxyrhynchus) and, on those grounds, was held by some to be of some kind of gnostic[2] origin. This view was gratefully seized upon by Christian scholars in particular, for it conveniently averted the threat which the thought system of Jesus poses to the Christian version of him—by dating the Thomas material as it does, much later than the canonical tradition. It was to be only much later that critical scholars of the textual tradition increasingly began to pay attention to the fact that, clearly, many sayings of Jesus seem to appear in their more original form in the Thomas gospel relative to the canonical literature of the New Testament (NT) and thus must have preceded it. The implications of that realization are only just now beginning to take effect.

While we did not have a complete text older than the Coptic

---

2 "Gnosis," or "gnosticism," is a term that has caused much confusion. In the religious melting pot of roughly three centuries after the death of Jesus, a fertile Middle Eastern mix of belief systems flourished, some of which have been designated with this terminology; yet, the classification has proven problematic. The term "gnosis," which means "knowledge," originally referred to an inspired inner knowing that is experiential, is beyond rational belief, and has the connotation of the complete certainty of spirit. Clearly, the later development of various sects, which leveraged the concept of "gnosis" into forms of secret knowledge and cult-like religions, complete with would-be initiations, was a deterioration of the concept: it became specific instead of abstract. By that time, we are talking about Gnosticism, as a religious phenomenon. Just because Jesus appeals to this inner knowing does not make him a gnostic in the sense of those baroque religions of the second and third centuries after his death. Nor is the Thomas gospel a gnostic work in that sense, for the term only makes any sense after ca. 100 CE.

manuscript with the 114 sayings from ca. 350 CE, there were fragments that were older, and the internal evidence suggests to a growing number of scholars that the Thomas gospel was collected in book form by ca. 50 CE, and therefore well before the other NT materials.[3] Clearly, it was subsequently suppressed by the nascent Church because it did not harmonize well with the then-emergent revisionist version of Jesus which was being developed by Paul, c.s., and which was becoming increasingly dominant (and domineering) during that time. The emergence of this "orthodoxy" ultimately led to the suppression and destruction of many materials that did not harmonize with this vision.

To clarify the nature and the time line of gnosticism a bit further, I would like to suggest that the word "gnosis" is just a word, one that should be read and understood independent from the religious forms that used the concept so prevalently in the second and third centuries CE. Today, the term "gnosis" is a descriptor of an inner knowing at a level below conscious thought, where all doubt simply is absent in the face of the certainty of inner experience, and where truth is true and everything else is a lie (e.g., ACIM:T-14.II.3:3-4), in particular, those "thoughts you think you think," as the Course humorously calls them (ACIM:W-15.1:1). It is the same notion as that which Socrates addressed in his teaching method, with his implicit reliance on the notion that the truth is within us and only needs to be uncovered.

"Gnosis" is also the rock of spiritual clarity and certainty upon which Jesus's true church is built, as he instructed the apostles with a playful pun on Simon's name, which means "listening," so that the implication is that listening to the Voice of the Holy Spirit

---

3   Greek fragments of the Thomas gospel had been found earlier in the Oxyrhynchus Papyrus, discovered at the end of the nineteenth century, and translations of it had been routinely available since the beginning of the twentieth century. These fragments were about 100-200 years older than the Coptic version.

is the only sure foundation, indeed "rock" solid (Greek *petra* = rock, hence the name Peter as a nickname for Simon). It should also be noted that this listening, as the Course constantly reminds us, means that we are accepting the gifts of the Spirit for ourselves first, as a precondition to passing them on in whatever situation we are in. It does not mean hearing voices and telling the neighbors what to do; it means listening and having the courage for ourselves to change teachers from the ego's urgent pressures to the Holy Spirit's loving guidance.

Several generations after Jesus's ministry, a confluence happened among Jewish mystical and wisdom traditions, as well as Greek and Middle Eastern mystery religions and philosophical imagination, in which the word "gnosis" now was given a new special meaning. This group of traditions has been collectively referred to as "gnosticism," because they all not only shared the prevalent use of this term, but also elaborated on it in sometimes fanciful ways that went far beyond the original meanings of the word. At times, the term became highly specific and technical in certain traditions and now might need to be distinguished as such with capitalization.

The fact that certain terms like "gnosis" later gain prevalence in the context of gnosticism is not grounds to label the Thomas gospel anachronistically as a gnostic—or even "gnosticising"—document, as some have done. This has been attempted by numerous scholars in a sort of logic of "guilt by association," which, however, does not hold water. Presently, a growing body of thought, including such scholars as the Jesus Seminar, are validating a more common-sense perception that the Thomas material does predate the other gospels which ended up in the NT Canon.

Today, the picture that has emerged is one in which Thomas and another "sayings" tradition, Q (the reader is referred to the Bibliography for source material on Q), as well as the Gospel of Mark, are considered to be the sources for the other two synoptic gospels in the NT Canon: Matthew and Luke.[4] And while I have followed enough of the literature over the years to be aware of this shift in thinking about the nature of the Thomas sayings, it was not until the treatment of them in Gary Renard's work that I came to appreciate the full implications of the Thomas sayings. From then on, spending time with these sayings has for me become an open invitation to spend time with Jesus and listen to his timeless message, which simply comes to different people in different forms at different times but, in essence, always remains the same.

The point of this observation is simply that this bit of early history of Christianity has become a lot clearer lately, and for students of the Course it reflects a psychological process with which we tend to become familiar during our own work with Jesus's teachings in the Course. This may take various forms, one of them being the ego's tendency to co-opt Jesus and so to end up studying the Course with the ego, becoming a "good Course student," which is exactly *not* the point. As Ken Wapnick (see Bibliography) relentlessly reminds us in his books, media material, and workshops, the point is to be a *lousy* Course student and forgive yourself for it, for it is that process which has us look with Jesus at our resistance to his presence in us. In other words, in modern terms the likes of Paul were the *good* students of their day, knowing Jesus's teachings and their meaning better than he did himself, subverting them with their "important" contributions. (As Jesus reminds us in the Course: "You are still convinced that your understanding is a powerful contribution to the truth, and makes it what it is." ACIM:T-18.IV.7:5) In this way, such

---

4   The synoptic gospels are commonly considered by scholars to be Mark, Matthew, and Luke. These gospels have a story-telling structure and deal more with the facts of Jesus's life on earth than with his teachings. This characterization is not necessarily helpful, though it is quite accepted. Matthew and Luke are certainly more characterized by this historical emphasis than is Mark. Mark is more abstract in tone, and though it is also in the form of a narrative, it deals only with Jesus's ministry. Arguably, less historical certainty may attach to Jesus's life before his ministry, however, and both Matthew and Luke use that part of the story to make their own points. (See Index 2 for details.)

propagandists, both then and now, adapt the teachings in the service of their own glory, thereby rendering them serviceable to the world and the ego. Through this fog of obfuscation, the world then loses touch with the direct message of such teachings. Along with this process comes the tendency of wanting to have Jesus do things for us in the world; i.e., miracles in the physical sense now take center stage as some sort of spectacle that would induce faith, when in fact the "change of mind" (the original and literal meaning of the original NT Greek word *metanoia*) which Jesus talked about, was and is the real miracle—then, now, and always. The ego's choice is always form over content, and so the literalistic, fundamentalist tradition which starts with Paul is an ego endeavor from day one, which paved the way for morphing Jesus's teachings into a world religion, suitable for service to Caesar (the ego).

Seen in that light, the implicit, yet central teaching point in the phenomenon of Gary Renard's two books is the connection of *A Course in Miracles* with the Gospel according to Thomas. This brings out the idea of the reality of Jesus as a timeless spiritual presence, by his very nature outside of time and space. After all, if the Jesus who taught two thousand years ago is the same Jesus who dictated the Course to Helen Schucman (see the section titled "On The Course" for details), he is hardly limited to the constraints of the experience of time and space which we hold to be our reality, the underlying point being that neither are we. Thus, Jesus can be present to every one of us whenever we call on him, and we join with his love outside of time and space whenever we choose the miracle. Another way of saying this is that Jesus is content, not form, and the reason we have so much trouble with this is because we are stuck in the assumption that form makes reality. If something does not have form, we think it is "only" an idea. But if the mind is reality and this world an illusion, we need to look at this again, which is what the Course is all about.

14

Within the context of the holographic model of the universe, which is emerging from quantum mechanics and which the Course espouses, we can understand better that Jesus is available to us as a presence in the mind[5] anytime we wish to open the door to him in our lives. In fact, that world of time and space is our own barrier against Jesus. As the Course says: "The world was made as an attack on God." (ACIM:W-pII.3.2:1). We speak here of the *resurrected* Jesus, very symbolically first recognized by his beloved Mary Magdalene, and not the *crucified* Jesus (the body, the character in the time/space world), who was made into an idol by a Christianity, which in turn had Mary Magdalene exit stage left. He is the Internal Teacher who, through the Course, would lead us home if we practice what he says. He is the Jesus who beckons the apostles to leave behind their accustomed roles and to follow him to a Kingdom not of this world. To me, Gary Renard's writing, and indeed his life, are a teaching example of this reality, and his books give concrete shape to it by demonstrating the inner consistency between now (*A Course in Miracles*) and then (Gospel of Thomas), as much as the fact that Gary himself is experiencing in the now the presence of parts of himself which are from the seeming past and the seeming future. Evidently, he demonstrates the undoing of the ego's substitute reality in those experiences. And he also makes no bones about sharing his fads and foibles with the readers, and never falls for the temptations of guru-hood, and posing as some enlightened teacher; rather, he presents himself as just another Course student, who is willing to share his experiences with his audience.

To do the topic justice, I want to explain here the principles on which this book is founded and the process of the book in order to provide total accountability for my method. While some may

---

5   The Course defines the term "mind" as "the activating agent of spirit, supplying
     its creative energy." (ACIM:C-1:1)

think that that is merely a standard scholarly formality, I consider it my responsibility as part of the job. After all, this is not a work of fiction, and I owe the reader an accounting of how I arrived at my conclusions, particularly since certain implied assumptions could be mistaken for carelessness in the absence of such clarification. The fact is that, in the accepted academic sense, it would not make any sense to use Pursah's version of the Gospel of Thomas as the authoritative text, but that is exactly what I am going to do here. Therefore, at the outset I have to acknowledge that my approach only makes sense to students of *A Course in Miracles* who, from their own experience, have no doubt that Jesus is speaking to us through its pages, and who can likewise accept the process by which Gary Renard subsequently wrote his books and recorded Pursah's authentic kernel of Gospel of Thomas in *Your Immortal Reality*. This current book is based on the assumption that Pursah's rendering of the Gospel of Thomas, for which she vouches that it is as close to the original as possible, is the best, most authoritative version.

To be precise, textual criticism is obviously of great value; however, it simply also has its limitations. First, in focusing always on form over content, it ultimately lacks any sure foundation in the spiritual sense; yet, historical context (form) is the only foundation textual scholars can more or less agree on. Quite obviously, it is the *content* of a book that counts when working with scriptural text. Unfortunately, it nearly universally is not (except in a superficial sense), the focus most often being limited to the *explicit* content at the expense of any deeper meaning (content), which would, of course, necessitate understanding what Jesus teaches. This entails following him in practice, for his teaching is to be known only through experience, not merely intellectually. In some respects, these are the mistakes of the Scribes and the Pharisees.[6] In the course of the present exploration, we will find interesting examples of the consequences of these shortcomings of the historical method.

Another related limitation becomes exposed by the very phenomena of *A Course in Miracles* and Gary Renard's books. To wit, what if a source arises out of the temporal sequence which, for valid reasons (or at least reasons acceptable to us), we find to be more authoritative as to content than certain temporally older texts? This is a violation of the established order of the Newtonian worldview, and thus it has no place in textual scholarship and history, but it is a violation which we will very consciously and deliberately permit ourselves here—not to mention feel good about, too! In short, I accept as a premise of this book the legitimacy of Pursah speaking from her past-life experience as the apostle Thomas, regarding the authentic and accurate form of the kernel of his gospel which she hands us in *Your Immortal Reality*.

The distinguishing feature in this process is the recognition that the dialectic mind by definition shuts itself out of Reality, which, as the Course teaches, is a non-dualistic Oneness that cannot be fathomed with words or philosophical or theological speculation, but can only be experienced.[7] For these very reasons,

---

6   Obviously, this reference to "Scribes and Pharisees" (who were the interpreters of the law at the time of Jesus) should not be read as denouncing certain groups; rather, it is meant to identify and point out a pernicious tendency from which most of us suffer, namely, elevating form over content, a favorite ego device.

7   The teaching of the Course is strictly non-dualistic at the highest level, though it also deals with our day-to-day experience in the world on a practical level. "Non-dualism" is often mischaracterized as a philosophical system. It is not. It is a parable for an experiential reality which escapes the dialectic mind altogether. Likewise, the Thomas sayings, as well as numerous sayings of Jesus from other traditions, only make sense in that light. Non-dualism is not monotheism and has naught to do with one God in lieu of many. To understand the inner meaning of "The Lord our God is One" is to understand non-dualism. The Course says: "We say 'God is,' and then we cease to speak, for in that knowledge words are meaningless." (ACIM:W-169.5:4) Non-dualism simply means that Reality is one and everything else is a lie, and "gods," either in the plural or singular, are projections that arise from the thought of separation, which is, however inherently an impossibility in a non-dualistic Reality and therefore an illusion. Words themselves, being dualistic by their very nature, cannot deal with this, but can only point to what experience alone can make real to us. By way of contrast, duality is separation from God, a world of opposites beginning with a distinction between subject and object, observer and observed.

no compromise is possible here, for dialectic reasoning will tend to invalidate the inner experience, which is the essence of the teachings of Jesus and the premise of a non-dualistic Reality. In other words, non-dualistic Reality defies intellectual understanding; it is known *only* through experience. And while it can be *hinted at* with words (as "pointers" to Reality, or *reflections* of Reality), it can never be conclusively *described* in words, since, as the Course puts it, "...words are but symbols of symbols. They are thus twice removed from reality." (ACIM:M-21.1:9-10)

Having accepted the above premises, the hierarchy of texts used in this book is very straightforward:

1 *Your Immortal Reality* (abbr. YIR), as the source for the authoritative text of Thomas, generally referred to as Pursah's Gospel of Thomas (abbr. P/GoTh), presented in Chapter 7 of the book;

2 The Gospel of Thomas (abbr. GoTh), of which I have consulted numerous translations, particularly the version of Prof. Marvin Meyer, with the special note that Arten and Pursah (see the section "Closing The Circle—Notes on Pursah's Gospel of Thomas") suggested this edition to Gary Renard as the preferred modern English translation before Pursah had given him the new text of her kernel of that gospel, which subsequently appeared in YIR (item 1 above); and

3 *The Disappearance of the Universe* (abbr. DU), for initial guidance on the interpretation and meaning of the twenty-two Thomas sayings discussed in it, as well as for the overall connection of the Thomas gospel to *A Course in Miracles*.

Besides the above, naturally *A Course in Miracles* itself, as well as the Bible and some extra-canonical literature to the NT, will be considered.

Along with these references, I must acknowledge the very special importance of the book *The Mythmaker: Paul and the Invention of Christianity*, by Hyam Maccoby. It is the most brilliant exposé that I have come across—and have had the pleasure to read—on the jarring disconnect between Paul and the actual teachings of Jesus. Many indeed have stumbled over various aspects of that inner contradiction in thought, but rarely if ever has there been such a systematic treatment of the topic. This book is the perfect corollary to a proper understanding of the pre-Pauline Jesus of the Thomas gospel as the teacher of a strictly non-dualistic teaching, which bore no likeness to the idolization of his person and his life on earth, which became the central tenet of Christianity. The Eucharist (the Church's sacramental rite of Holy Communion), the notion of Jesus's exclusivity as the Son of God (God's *only* Son), the bodily resurrection, the interpretation of the Second Coming, vicarious salvation and its sacrificial theology, the idolization of suffering, the theology of sin/guilt/fear which is implicit in the idea of Jesus's dying for our sins (vicarious salvation), and the need to proselytize—all these concepts go back to Paul, not Jesus, so that none of what makes Christianity what it is, as a separate religion, can be attributed to Jesus at all.

I would tend to disagree with Maccoby only in that I feel Jesus's teachings definitely did transcend Judaism and were *de facto* universal in their meaning. Nonetheless, it is now becoming a matter of historical honesty to understand that Christianity is a Pauline invention which merely quotes Jesus, but hardly represents him. It is interesting to note that attentive students of the Bible do come to question Paul from time to time; yet, ultimately they virtually always vindicate him in the ensuing theological debates. No one seems to notice that this is perhaps less a testimony to the relevance of Paul to Jesus's teachings than to the fact that, if Christianity was invented by Paul, a Christian theologian would necessarily have to reaffirm his position. As such, the validation of Paul's teachings about Jesus by his spiritual heirs is tautological and still says nothing about his accuracy in representing Jesus. The historically more accurate view simply would acknowledge that Christianity merely is a world religion which claims Jesus as its source, as distinct from representing his teachings. In Appendix 1, there is a reprint of a letter written by Thomas Jefferson, in which he gives singularly strong expression to this feeling of doubt around the legitimacy of Paul's teaching. Naturally, Jefferson's opinion has not received much of an audience today, and he mostly kept it to himself during his lifetime, since many people might not have appreciated his feelings on the matter at that time.

In flippantly modern terms, one could sum up the situation as follows: the Jesus of Christianity is a private-label version of Jesus, made-to-order by Paul of Tarsus, using his charisma to popularize Jesus and to develop his teaching into a religion that was new and different from Judaism and all other religious forms of the contemporary Middle East. We should note that the making of Christianity into something unique and special was a neurotic need of Paul and his associates and was never expressed by Jesus, who clearly spoke his truth to anyone who would come to him, completely disregarding any prejudice based on ethnic or religious affiliations. Jesus spoke in a universal way. But, again, Paul's revisionism made Jesus and Christianity unique and so gave form to the ego's need for specialness, not to the ageless and universal spirituality that Jesus taught.

From the perspective of the teachings of *A Course in Miracles*, the Pauline reconstruction of Jesus's teachings and reinterpretation of his life throughout rests on "level confusion," a term by which the Course describes the ego's insistence on interpreting on level two (the dualistic world of time and space) what can only be understood on level one (the abstract world of spirit). The express purpose of this ego tactic is to make the world real by keeping our attention engaged in seeking the cause of everything on level two; in this way, we reinforce the blocks that prevent us from realizing that our reality is strictly on level one and, therefore, that the cause of anything is only in the mind. Thus the ego would ensure that we continuously "Seek but do not find." (ACIM:T-16.V.6:5)— the 180-degree opposite of what Jesus taught.

The so-called "mysteries of the faith" then arise as a result of fitting a non-dualistic square peg into a dualistic round hole and are revealed to be merely the taboos the ego uses to ensure that we never question its assumptions, as they rest on nothing. If we were to bring them to light, as the Course has us do, ultimately we would of necessity have to come back to the mind (level one) in undoing the ego's reversal of cause and effect, which, until then, keeps us in a state of permanent confusion.

The following texts from the Course make explicit the notion that Jesus wanted to share his mind—not his body—with us...

The Holy Spirit, Who leads to God, translates communication into being, just as He ultimately translates perception into knowledge. You do not lose what you communicate. The ego uses the body for attack, for pleasure and for pride. The insanity of this perception makes it a fearful one indeed. The Holy Spirit sees the body only as a means of communication, and because communicating is sharing, it becomes communion. Perhaps you think that fear as well as love can be communicated; and therefore can be shared. Yet this is not so real as it may appear. Those who communicate fear are promoting attack, and attack always breaks communication, making it impossible. Egos do join together in temporary allegiance, but always for what each one can get *separately*. The Holy Spirit communicates only what each one can give to all. He never takes anything back, because He wants you to keep it. Therefore, His teaching begins with the lesson: *To have, give all to all.* (ACIM:T-6.V.A.5)

...and that this sharing of his mind—not his body—is the true meaning of communion, rather than the somewhat cannibalistic ritual that Christianity made of it:

> You cannot forget the Father because I am with you, and I cannot forget Him. To forget me is to forget yourself and Him Who created you. Our brothers are forgetful. That is why they need your remembrance of me and of Him Who created me. Through this remembrance, you can change their minds about themselves, as I can change yours. Your mind is so powerful a light that you can look into theirs and enlighten them, as I can enlighten yours. I do not want to share my body in communion because this is to share nothing. Would I try to share an illusion with the most holy children of a most holy Father? Yet I do want to share my mind with you because we are of one Mind, and that Mind is ours. See only this Mind everywhere, because only this is everywhere and in everything. It is everything because it encompasses all things within itself. Blessed are you who perceive only this, because you perceive only what is true. (ACIM:T-7.V.10)

Also, early Christianity overwhelmingly saw the *imitatio Christi* as copying Jesus's (seeming) human suffering and persecution (see also the discussion of Logion 9 in the section "The Logia"). In contrast, the Course suggests his point was to teach that he did not suffer, since his mind was at perfect peace ("Father forgive them for they know not what they do." ACIM:T-2.V.A.16.3), as he *knew* he was not his body, and *that* is what he wanted us to learn and copy. Accordingly, Jesus in the Course clarifies:

> You are not persecuted, nor was I. You are not asked to repeat my experiences because the Holy Spirit, Whom we share, makes this unnecessary. To use my experiences constructively, however, you must still follow my example in how to perceive them. My brothers and yours are constantly engaged in justi-

22

fying the unjustifiable. My one lesson, which I must teach as I learned it, is that no perception that is out of accord with the judgment of the Holy Spirit can be justified. I undertook to show this was true in an extreme case, merely because it would serve as a good teaching aid to those whose temptation to give in to anger and assault would not be so extreme. I will with God that none of His Sons should suffer. (ACIM:T-6.I.11)

What he means is that when somebody steps on your toes (preferably figuratively, if you should have any choice in the matter), then forgive him, and you will be teaching that person *and yourself* that you are not a body. Surely having someone step on your toes is not as extreme an example as the crucifixion, and we would do well to remind ourselves of this from time to time in the course of our daily forgiveness opportunities.

Perhaps in a way not too dissimilar from what Paul did in founding Christianity from the teachings of Jesus, there are writers today who use *A Course in Miracles* in their teachings— and some of them have seemingly been the greatest popularizers of the Course—who do not necessarily teach what it says in all its aspects. In one case, this kind of popularity unwittingly caused widespread confusion about the authorship of the Course: I have had to answer questions more than once from people who thought that Marianne Williamson wrote the Course, and I even once had to help a bookstore place an order for the Course, since they could not find *A Course in Miracles* under the name of this author. A similar problem exists with many others who use the Course in their teaching and writing but introduce other elements into it or otherwise compromise its message. In this book, I have taken great effort in staying true to the Course, and any deviations from its teaching are my mistakes. A detailed Bibliography is provided in the back.

A further point worthy of note is the relationship of the Thomas gospel to the Synoptics in particular, because this is what has led many scholars to believe that the Thomas gospel *de facto* pre-existed the Synoptics in close to its present form. Most significantly, this implies that it also predates Paul, whose editorial influence is present in all three gospels (regarding interpretation of the Eucharist, for example), though perhaps somewhat less in Mark. Note that Luke and Matthew are more contemporaneous and similar to each other, while Luke and Acts were originally one book, which was written by Paul's assistant. Pursah also pays attention to this issue in identifying certain Thomas sayings as "prequels" to the NT. (See DU pp. 79-80, and Index 2 in this book.) My principal source for issues relating to Mark has been the volume *The Gospel of Mark* in *The New International Greek Testament Commentary* series (see Bibliography), besides the Greek text and the usual translations. As to other sources regarding Thomas, the website for this book is www.acimnthomas.com and it has a link to a blog at www.xanga.com/rogierfvv, which is dedicated solely to discussing materials related to this book, starting with the references listed in the Bibliography of this book, the purpose of which is to provide detail that might be overkill in this book itself, and which will also provide eventual subsequent elaborations to the postings.

To summarize the current research and harmonize it with Pursah's views, it would appear that the kernel of Thomas which Pursah represents as authentic was "together" in some primitive form ca. 50 CE, but gradually accumulated other sayings, embellishments, and corruptions. Ultimately, it evolved into the book of 114 sayings that we see reflected partially in the Greek fragments of the Oxyrhynchus Papyrus (ca. 150-250 CE), and finally in full form in the Nag Hammadi find, which is estimated to date from about 150 years after the Greek papyri.[8] Its burial probably coincided with the establishment of the NT Canon (under Bishop Athanasius in 367 CE). The Church now became more and more institutionalized and, along with that, less tolerant, which resulted in the purging and suppression of literature, such as the Thomas gospel and the rest of the Nag Hammadi materials, since they came to be regarded as heretical, pursuant to the judgment of them as being "extra-canonical" or "apocryphal." In the context of the work of Gary Renard, we should probably surmise that Pursah is suggesting that her rendition of Thomas is the "original" version of no later than ca. 50 CE.

What is crucial to understand, in particular to us as students of the Course, is that the typical theological constructs that were later to make Christianity what it became were not present in the early traditions—neither the "Q" tradition, nor the Thomas sayings. Next, there is the general logic that the history of quoting Jesus's sayings in the Synoptics strongly suggests that the older forms are in Thomas because they acquire subsequent enhancements in the synoptic tradition. Also, there are more indirect clues to the date of the Thomas gospel, such as Logion 12, which suggests to the apostles that they rely on James after Jesus is gone, an argument which would not make much sense after the death of James in 62 CE. In other words, this saying suggests, from a perspective of historical coherence, that it was added to the collection sometime before 62 CE in order to make any sense at all—leaving aside the question of whether or not Jesus actually said it, which Pursah evidently feels he did not, since she skips this saying altogether. It could easily have been a spurious and self-serving addition by a member of the James community, but, even so, this would still tend to support the early dating.

In all, there is plenty of common-sense evidence here as to why the basic Thomas gospel dates from the first generation following Jesus's death and most importantly from a time before

---

8   The first find of Greek fragments of the Thomas gospel was at Oxyrhynchus, in Egypt, at the end of the nineteenth century. The find at Nag Hammadi, also in Egypt, was a Coptic manuscript, which was originally discovered in 1945. It took a while after that before it was translated and became available in book form.

the theological influence of Paul. The tendency among scholars of dating the final form later depends in part on the dating of the Oxyrhynchus Papyrus, and in part on the notion of presumed gnostic influences in Thomas, which are considered to be of a later date, closer to the likely composition date of the Oxyrhynchus Papyrus. This concern about gnostic thought anachronistically hinges upon the whole issue of the emergent Pauline orthodoxy, which rejects gnostic influences as heresy. While this world view puts us all down as miserable sinners, it should be clear that, in that condition, we could most certainly not be endowed with a right mind. And our innate capacity for that inner knowing, or gnosis, is the crucial notion to which the teachings of Jesus appeal, then and now. For those of us who are comfortable with the Jesus of *A Course in Miracles*, it is easy to see why many themes of the thought system which Jesus represents could easily flow into gnosticism and in fact how some gnostic sources very likely reflect certain aspects of Jesus's teaching very faithfully, such as, for example, the influential second-century gnostic Christian teacher Valentinus. For an in-depth exploration of these issues, the reader is referred to Ken Wapnick's *Love Does Not Condemn* (see Bibliography).

When these historical relationships are considered, the idea that the original teachings of Jesus as reflected in the Thomas source should be consistent with the teachings of *A Course in Miracles*, as suggested by Pursah, would seem to make complete logical sense. And it could be almost an Aha! moment for many who have wondered why the Jesus of Thomas sounds more like a Buddhist than a Christian.

A concluding comment about Jesus is in order. Starting immediately with Paul, a dualistic teaching around Jesus—a reconstruction of Jesus, to be sure—began to develop, in which the "change of mind" (Gr. *metanoia*) that Jesus taught became a moral "repentance" or "conversion," something which seems to range from the bi-polar flight into health—to use a Freudian term[9]—as Paul experienced, to a calculated conversion to a circumscribed set of beliefs about him, which was later cast in stone in the form of the Nicene Creed (325 CE). In other words, the non-dualistic teaching, which was geared to experience of the truth by following Jesus (out of this world) in order to seek and find his Kingdom (not of this world), was brought down into the dialectic mind and turned into a product of recursive thinking and moral deliberation, as a would-be compass to navigate in the world. Thus it is brought into the realm of what the Buddhists refer to as "monkey-mind" and what the Course calls "the thoughts you think you think"(ACIM:W-15.1:1) because their referent is the ego and because they are mere epiphenomena of our real thoughts, which are creative. These ego thoughts are geared very much to existing in this world and concerned with making distinctions between right and wrong, good and bad. In the process, Jesus is reduced from his reality as an ever-present Internal Teacher, accessible in spirit always, residing in our inner reality outside of time and space, and given a role in the drama of the world. In further developments, the reality of Jesus was increasingly buried in a new symbolism and mythology developed around him. These gradual developments focused more and more on Jesus's life in the world, his body, and his crucifixion, and buried completely the non-dualistic, level-one meaning of his teachings.

We might note that, later in the evolution of the Church, the energy and proximate cause of the Reformation no doubt was Luther's outrage at the selling of indulgences by the Church, but the substance of it was his conviction that people should have their own relationship with Jesus and with God, a notion to

---

9 Students of the Course will recognize this issue. The term "flight into health" was coined by Sigmund Freud to describe how a patient will often end his therapy prematurely, by pretending a miracle recovery, exactly because he does not want to let go of his reasons for his problems, which is an unconscious defense mechanism. At various stages of the Course path, this phenomenon can manifest as "blissninnyhood" (as Ken Wapnick has labeled it), a condition of pretend-happiness which, in the end, is merely another layer of denial.

which he gave form in his translation of the Bible into the German vernacular, having conveniently been provided with the means to divulge it by the contemporaneous appearance of the printing press. The degree of mythologizing around Jesus in the Catholic Church thus started to become more and more exposed, and, by the nineteenth century, radical Protestant theologians increasingly sought a more solid foundation for their faith. Understandably, if naively, that began with searching for the Jesus of history, thus overcompensating for the gross distortions of the Catholic Church. The result was yet again an overemphasis on Jesus's life on earth over the teachings of Jesus, though periodically there were flare-ups in the debate in which indeed the question was raised as to what extent Paul distorted the teachings of Jesus.

The latter concern was particularly prevalent in the school of Radikalkritik[10] in Germany and Holland. Another interesting example of this line of thinking is to be found in the book *The Christ Myth,* by Arthur Drews (see Bibliography). And we see similar sentiments in some of Thomas Jefferson's commentary cited above. I have already expressed my view that the finest and most hard-hitting and definitive commentary to be found is the much more recent book by Hyam Maccoby, *The Mythmaker: Paul and the Invention of Christianity.* However, in looking back at this history, it is very interesting to see that the urge to find the real Jesus once and for all produced a bifurcation between some who became engrossed in the provable historical aspects of the life of Jesus, and others who ended up declaring Jesus a myth completely. Some authors, at least in better moments, used the

---

10 Radikalkritik was a current of thought in nineteenth- and twentieth-century German and Dutch Protestant theology which focused on doubting the legitimacy of the NT letters of Paul categorically and questioning the historicity of Jesus. The best source of information on the topic may be www.hermann-detering.de. The development goes back to the English theologian Edward Evanson (1731-1805), who in 1892 published *The dissonance of the four generally received evangelists and the evidence of their respective authenticity,* in which the foundation is laid. In Germany, it was perhaps Hegel's pupil Bruno Bauer (1809-1882) who questioned the letters of Paul categorically as products of evident self-justification of emergent Christianity of the second century.

notion of a mythical Jesus with an appreciation for the fact that this idea might even be constructive to our spiritual appreciation and understanding of him (e.g., Arthur Drews). In other words, while some saw the "Jesus myth" theme as a way of debunking the faith in him, others appreciated that he had a symbolic importance which substantially exceeded any physical reality, so that the historicity of Jesus is exactly *not* the point.

Roughly a hundred years later, after their liberation by Vatican II, Catholic scholars began to join the stampede in the search for the historical Jesus. I have heard rumors of dissent regarding the issue of the fissure between Jesus and Paul among some in the clergy, but I know of little external evidence of such discussion, which is not surprising, given the repressive nature of the institution. But what you deny you project (see later footnote on "projection"), and so, in this particular case the doubts do seem to have found an outlet in such phenomena as *The Da Vinci Code* and a whole host of other literature which may be of dubious scholarly value, but which cleverly feeds on the innate sense of betrayal by the Church. This kind of development comes with the territory of being a would-be spiritual authority in the world—a complete *non-sequitur* to begin with for attentive readers who notice that Jesus maintained that "my Kingdom is not of this earth," as indeed the very word "spiritual" would seem to imply. The Church is also eager to assist in its own demise by taking such books seriously and defending themselves against them.

Meanwhile, the spreading of *A Course in Miracles*, and the fact that Gary Renard's books have made the best-seller lists with such rapidity and stayed there for long periods of time, demonstrate clearly that the world is ready to look at things in quite a different way from the traditional Christian fare. It seems to me indeed that the role of churches in the future would almost have to become more and more of a social nature and less and less prescriptive of specific beliefs other than core values, as well as accepting if not encouraging of their membership to seek out their own spiritual truth, rather than be forced into any particular canned beliefs. Some churches play a very positive role in facilitating inquiry and hosting workshops on a wide variety of spiritual teachings and religious practices, sometimes even on *A Course in Miracles.*

As to the use of the name Jesus, we may note that in *A Course in Miracles,* Jesus is the implied author, but he does not make a big fuss about what we call him. He presents himself both as our "elder brother" (cf. ACIM:T-1.II.3:7) and as a "symbol for the Holy Spirit." In Gary Renard's books, the abbreviation "J" is used to remove some potential obstacles that some people may feel. Personally, I was brought up with the notion of "God's Help" (which is the meaning of the Hebrew name JeHoShua, or Joshua) as a presence we can always call on, as long as we are willing to accept his Help on *his* terms, not ours—in other words, he is not a wish-fulfilling Santa Claus. That distinction is very similar to the notion in *A Course in Miracles,* that we need to come up to Jesus's level instead of bringing him down to ours, as Christianity did. The expression the Course uses for this notion is to "bring the question to the answer" (cf. ACIM:T-27.IV.7:5), instead of the other way around. The central point is that we cannot have our cake and eat it too; we cannot make the problem real *and* have the Answer, so the condition of the Answer is that we "follow him" to his Kingdom not of this world, and with him we can look upon ourselves in this life and come to a different point of view. In my own experience, that notion of God's Help sort of straddles the fence between the abstract "Holy Spirit" and the personalized "Jesus," and the point is whatever works for you is fine—Jesus, Buddha, Quan Yin, Krishna, or even "J," or your own personal variation.

On The Course

This section is intended for readers who are not yet (?) familiar with *A Course in Miracles*. It provides a brief recap of the history of the Course as well as some core concepts, without attempting to be exhaustive. Serious readers will want to consult the source materials for themselves.

A Course in Miracles (a.k.a., "ACIM," or "the Course") is perhaps best characterized as a self-study program for spiritual growth, in which Jesus ("J" in Gary Renard's work) is the therapist. Jesus in the Course is a symbolic figure in our life who represents to us our innate capability to remember our true nature as spirit and live accordingly. The Course also refers to Jesus as "the manifestation of the Holy Spirit,"[11] and the Holy Spirit, in turn, is viewed by the Course as our memory of the truth (which remained with us when we thought we separated from God), as opposed to the illusory substitute reality we imagine to be our life.[12]

Jesus (or "J," if you prefer) firmly planted his footsteps for us to follow in, so that we will eventually remember, as he did, who/what we really are as spirit, the one Son of God, and thereby find our way back home. This very literally is what he means by "following him." It is neither about preaching nor about

---

11 Cf. ACIM:C-6.1:1: Jesus is the manifestation of the *Holy Spirit*, Whom he called down upon the earth after he ascended into Heaven, or became completely identified with the Christ, the Son of God as He created Him.
12 Cf. ACIM:T-13.XI.11: The Holy Spirit will undo for you everything you have learned that teaches that what is not true must be reconciled with truth. This is the reconciliation the ego would substitute for your reconciliation to sanity and to peace. The Holy Spirit has a very different kind of reconciliation in His Mind for you, and one He will effect as surely as the ego will not effect what it attempts. Failure is of the ego, not of God. From Him you cannot wander, and there is no possibility that the plan the Holy Spirit offers *to* everyone, for the salvation *of* everyone, will not be perfectly accomplished. You will be released, and you will not remember anything you made that was not created for you and by you in return. For how can you remember what was never true, or not remember what has always been? It is this reconciliation with truth, and only truth, in which the peace of Heaven lies.

mouthing beliefs about him; it is always about the experience and about doing what he says, not saying what he does. The learning occurs when we realize that the steps we take are the steps he took, until we fully realize our oneness with him. We learn to generalize the lessons he has shown us in his life, including the extreme example of the crucifixion, and learn to apply them in the less extreme circumstances of our own life. In other words, within the context of the specifics of our own life, we come to understand the content of what he taught us by demonstrating that he knew he was not his body. Thereby, we undo our own choice for the crucifixion (figuratively speaking) step by step and choose to accept the Atonement instead. (See the section "The Message of the Crucifixion" in Chapter 6 of the Course.)

The method of the Course is centered around a profound understanding of the psychological principle of "projection,"[13] and an equally sophisticated process of "advanced forgiveness" (see Logion 58 in the section "The Logia") as a way to undo those projections (illusions) and choose the Atonement instead—the Atonement being the acceptance of Reality where no separation ever happened, and therefore the denial and ultimately the complete forgetting of the dream-world in which we think we live. It should be noted that the Course's idea of atonement (or salvation) is "Atonement without sacrifice," since we are giving up nothing (the ego's illusion of a world) for everything (the Peace of God). (Note especially ACIM:T-3.I.)

In this context, it is important to understand that the Course's cosmogenesis holds that what we are is spirit, a thought in the Mind of God:

---

13 The psychological defense mechanism of "projection" is another concept that was brought to the world's attention by Sigmund Freud. The Course takes it completely literally, and it is a major principle used in the Course to describe how we automatically and unconsciously project outward what is denied within and thereby make up the substitute reality of our world and the pseudo-realities of individual existence. On a macro-level, it is thus the equivalent of the "Big Bang" of modern astrophysics. As the Course puts it: "Projection makes perception." (e.g. ACIM:T-13.V.3:5)

Nothing that God knows not exists. And what He knows exists forever, changelessly. For thoughts endure as long as does the mind that thought of them. And in the Mind of God there is no ending, nor a time in which His Thoughts were absent or could suffer change. Thoughts are not born and cannot die. They share the attributes of their creator, nor have they a separate life apart from his. The thoughts you think are in your mind, as you are in the Mind which thought of you. And so there are no separate parts in what exists within God's Mind. It is forever One, eternally united and at peace. (ACIM:T-30.III.6)

We are created by God as spirit, as his one Son, his natural extension, but in oneness with Him in which there is no thought of individuality separate from Him. In the following paragraph in the Course, we are given an explanation for the unexplainable, namely, that the separation never really happened in the first place; it is only our *belief* in it which (seems to) make it so:

Into eternity, where all is one, there crept a tiny, mad idea, at which the Son of God remembered not to laugh. In his forgetting did the thought become a serious idea, and possible of both accomplishment and real effects. (ACIM:T-27.VIII. 6:2-3)

And so, a fundamental notion in the Course is that the world is not made by God, but rather is a manifestation—a "miscreation" (to use the Course's term)—which arises from the ego thought of separation, which the Course refers to as the "tiny, mad idea," in notable contrast to the importance the world attaches to the notion of individuality. It is a question of the observer and the observed: the phenomenon is not there until the observer chooses to see things that way.

Thus, salvation[14] is the denial of the separation and an experiential realization of the memory of Heaven, which Jesus personified and lived by. Following his example in deed, not in word, allows us also to live in the full knowing that this world is not our home (to be *in* the world, but not *of* it), and that in truth we are denizens of the "Kingdom not of this world," of which "J" speaks in the tradition but which has been thoroughly misunderstood to take place some time off in the distant future. As the Course puts it in the Introduction: "...awareness of love's presence...is our natural inheritance," and, in that context, our job is merely to remove the obstacles to this presence of love. In other words, salvation is reality, for nothing did happen, except we do not know it yet. In reality, therefore, salvation is to be found in the eternal now, merely by dropping our identification with a separate self that seems to lead our so-called "life" in the substitute reality of time and space, but which is merely our defense against the reality of what we really are. Within the ego thought system, which we mistake for our reality, it is our flight from this present reality for which we use time.[15] Salvation in this sense is thus the only meaningful choice we have here, the choice being between dreams and reality.

And so, the way "J" — the protagonist in the Course — speaks to us from its pages is as spirit, capable of remembering our home in Heaven, even if we are temporarily lost. And, again, he is there for us as our "elder brother" (cf. ACIM:T-1.II.3:7) who can guide us purely because he has gone before and can show us the way whenever we ask him. The purpose of the Course is to offer us an

---

14 In the context of the Course, the concept of "salvation" is the idea that nothing happened, and our seeming separation from God is an illusion that we can merely laugh away by learning to see it for what it is, but with forgiving, nonjudgmental eyes, thus taking the wind out of the sails of the ego. By contrast, the ego idea of salvation arises from the *belief* that the separation is real and serious, we are therefore guilty of sin, something needs to be done, and salvation can only be found outside of us.

15 Cf. ACIM:W158.4.1. Time is a trick, a sleight of hand, a vast illusion in which figures come and go as if by magic.

intellectually coherent presentation, along with a Workbook of 365 lessons, which are meant to be done "one a day" for a year and designed to lead us to an inner experience of the truth Jesus represents. On this path, he is present to us as our "Internal Teacher," as the Course calls him in the Preface.

The upshot of all this is that the Jesus of the Course clearly does not recognize any of the tenets of Christianity, which distinguished it as a religion different from Judaism in particular. Vicarious salvation, the Eucharist, and the Resurrection of the body, as well as the Second Coming as a future event (as Christianity sees it), let alone the Nicene Creed, are all out. However, the Course leverages the concepts of the Judaeo/Christian culture for the simple reason that it is the dominant tradition of the West, and Jesus very deliberately uses many familiar Christian terms in the Course but gives them a new meaning. Even if certain traditions might have previously sought to express some similar understandings to a degree, never before have those teachings been presented in such a coherent, comprehensive, and consistent way as in the Course. Thus, "Atonement" in the Course means not sacrifice, but rather the realization that there is no sin (since the separation never happened in the first place—we only *believe* that it did), and the "Resurrection" is the awakening of the mind to the realization that, indeed, we are mind from Mind and never left Heaven to begin with. (Cf. an earlier footnote on "salvation" and a subsequent one on "the Second Coming," as well as comments on "forgiveness" with Logion 58.)

As this book will show, the aforementioned teachings of the Course connect very well with the teachings of "J" in the Thomas gospel. The only difference between the Jesus of two thousand years ago and the Jesus of the Course today is that, within the historical framework, the arrival of such notions as Sigmund Freud's psychoanalysis and the works of William Shakespeare, as well as the holographic model of the universe that is emerging from quantum mechanics, prepared the way for the Course and provides the context for a richer and more direct and understandable way of teaching than the veiled metaphoric language of the Jesus who speaks to us from the Logia in the Thomas gospel.

*

Gary Renard's most recent book, *Your Immortal Reality*, summarizes some of the defining concepts of the Course, a few of which I am using here for this recapitulation, along with some additional comments, as follows:

- "There is no world! This is the central thought the course attempts to teach." (ACIM:W-132.6:2-3) This is to say that the manifest universe is purely illusory and an outflow only of the "tiny, mad idea," which can seem to exist only as long as we entertain the separation thought. In other words, it is the projection of an idea into form, which is sustained only by our *belief* in it.

- "The body does not exist except as a learning device for the mind. This learning device is not subject to errors of its own, because it cannot create. It is obvious, then, that inducing the mind to give up its miscreations is the only application of creative ability that is truly meaningful." (ACIM:T-2.V.1:9-11) This explains the body as only an effect of thoughts in the mind, and the body can be useful to us on our way home if we accept the Holy Spirit's purpose for it instead of our own "tiny, mad idea" of separation. It points out the Newtonian error of seeing the body as the cause of everything or anything at all. It is only an effect, and in that recognition lies our freedom from slavery to the body and the world of time and space. It should be noted that "the body" in the Course encompasses all of our bodies as traditional esoteric thought has recognized them—astral, etheric, mental, and physical—including, therefore, everything from the idea of individuality down to its physical manifestation, which is commonly referred to as our "body."

- The central teaching, which helps us undo the ego thought system, is Jesus's teaching of forgiveness, in which our choice for conflict can be replaced with a choice for peace, as expressed here: "The holiest of all the spots on earth is where an ancient hatred has become a present love." (ACIM:T-26.IX.6:1) That miracle is a core concept of the Course, as the name of the book indicates.

- As we choose the path of learning to which Jesus invites us, "Their readiness will bring the lesson to them in some form which they can understand and recognize." (ACIM:W:132.7:2) This says that in accepting the Holy Spirit's purpose, our life is seen as a series of classrooms in which we can learn to find our way back to the truth which Jesus represents to us, and his Course is a detailed instruction book on this path. Crucially, we do not have to decamp to a mountaintop in the Himalayas for a life of seclusion in order to find God; our relationships in this life, right here and now, are the path to salvation if we accept the Holy Spirit, not the ego, as our guide. Indeed, escaping from those relationships to a degree deprives our Internal Teacher of the very classroom in which our lessons are practiced and learned, and would constitute a detour that makes the journey longer, not shorter, being simply yet another judgment we have to undo.

- "What is not love is murder. What is not loving must be an attack. Every illusion is an assault on truth, and every one does violence to the idea of love because it seems to be of equal truth." (ACIM:T-23.IV.1:10-12) Learning to see that the thought of separation, the ego, always gets us into trouble is the essential foundation of the Course's teaching, since it is the *conditio sine qua non* of making the "other" choice, for the thought system of the Holy Spirit. After all, as long as you do not know you are in trouble, why change at all?

• By contrast, love represents oneness, which is our natural condition, and the miracle is the changing of our mind from the ego thought system to that of the Holy Spirit, thus dramatically altering our experience in this life. One of the first statements in the Course, "Miracle Principle" number one, makes this point very explicitly: "All expressions of love are maximal." (ACIM:T-1.I.1:4)

• A central point of the Course is the possibility of changing our mind and undoing the tangle. This means we have a direct responsibility for our salvation. This choice is easy in the end, for it turns out to be a simple choice between illusions and reality. Thus, the outcome of the process is inevitable, because reality could never be changed in the first place. Another key Course quote which *Your Immortal Reality* cites is: "Awareness of dreaming is the real function of God's teachers." (ACIM:M-12.6:6) What this says is that enlightened living is not to not have an ego, but to not take it seriously.

• And here come a few more "definitive ideas" as quoted in *Your Immortal Reality*:

   - "The secret of salvation is but this: that you are doing this unto yourself." (ACIM:T-27.VIII.10:1)

   - "The world you see is an illusion of a world. God did not create it, for what He creates must be eternal as Himself." (ACIM:C.4.1:1-2)

- "Whatever is true is eternal, and cannot change or be changed. Spirit is therefore unalterable because it is already perfect, but the mind can elect what it chooses to serve. The only limit put on its choice is that it cannot serve two masters." (ACIM:T-1.V.5:1-3)

- ...and then comes the crux of Jesus's teaching of forgiveness: "Forgiveness recognizes what you thought your brother did to you has not occurred. It does not pardon sins and make them real. It sees there was no sin. And in that view are all your sins forgiven." (ACIM:W-pII.1.1:1-4) It is important to realize that this does not mean denial of the facts (which would be less than helpful), but denial of our *interpretation* of them, in which the ego always presents itself as the referent, thus biasing us to take everything personally, ensuring that we maintain the conflict on the "battlefield" of this world, which is very reminiscent of the imagery in the Bhagavad Gita. The point is that, if we remember who we really are, the conflict is non-existent.

- I would like to add to this list a key passage from the Course section on "The Dreamer of the Dream," which Arten and Pursah (see the following section, "Closing The Circle— Notes on Pursah's Gospel of Thomas") at one point during their conversations with Gary recommended that he read entirely five times in succession over a period of a few months (see YIR p. 115). The second paragraph says this:

Now you are being shown you *can* escape. All that is needed is you look upon the problem as it is, and not the way that you have set it up. How could there be another way to solve a problem that is very simple, but has been obscured by heavy clouds of complication, which were made to keep the problem unresolved? Without the clouds the problem will emerge in all its primitive simplicity. The choice will not be difficult, because the problem is absurd when clearly seen. No one has difficulty making up his mind to let a simple problem be resolved if it is seen as hurting him, and also very easily removed. (ACIM:T-27.VII.2)

- Finally, to understand the Course's Miracle Principle number one, "There is no order of difficulty in miracles."(ACIM:T-1.I.1:1), is to understand the Course.

The above is, to all intents and purposes, a recap of a recap, an ultra-condensed summarization of some of the main teaching points of the Course in line with Chapter 4 of *Your Immortal Reality*, and it is provided here only to assist those who are not yet familiar with that material. If the brevity of this presentation makes you feel as if you really should read the source material, that is to be expected. After all, if you got this far, you probably should. The most helpful thing I could say is that *The Disappearance of the Universe*, which reads like a whodunit, is *de facto* a complete recap of, and introduction to, the Course. There are other options, some of which you may find in the Bibliography in this book.

To summarize the Course in yet a different way, with a more philosophical statement, we could say that it is a non-dualistic teaching clad in the metaphor of our dualistic experience in this life. In the following key paragraph from Chapter 1, section II, of the Course, Jesus (or "J"), who is clearly evident as the "I" who speaks the Course, points out to us that there is nothing he has that we do not have and the only difference between him and us is time:

Awe should be reserved for revelation, to which it is perfectly and correctly applicable. It is not appropriate for miracles because a state of awe is worshipful, implying that one of a lesser order stands before his Creator. You are a perfect creation, and should experience awe only in the Presence of the Creator of perfection. The miracle is therefore a sign of love among equals. Equals should not be in awe of one another because awe implies inequality. It is therefore an inappropriate reaction to me. An elder brother is entitled to respect for his greater experience, and obedience for his greater wisdom. He is also entitled to love because he is a brother, and to devotion if he is devoted. It is only my devotion that entitles me to yours. There is nothing about me that you cannot attain. I have nothing that does not come from God. The difference between us now is that I have nothing else. This leaves me in a state which is only potential in you. (ACIM:T-1.II.3)

Thus, again in the language of metaphor—which is the only thing we can understand as long as we are identified with our ego-self and its substitute life—if we follow Jesus (as per the biblical word, "To the apostles individually he explained everything." cf. Mark 4:34), he will lead us to his Kingdom not of this world, i.e., out of our dualistic world. It is through experience alone that we can learn to remember our non-dualistic reality, which transcends words (words are dualistic, after all), and the path that he teaches us in the Course revolves around forgiveness of the imaginary slights the world seems to inflict on us.

The Course points out that the conflicts on the "battleground" of this, our imaginary life, merely serve as reinforcement of our identity as a seemingly separated self and the dream-life it leads, because the conflicts we experience in our daily life have this ego-identity as a referent and keep us rooted in the experience of separation, which is the very thing that makes us miserable in the first place. Salvation is thus a change of mind, or *"metanoia"* (NT Greek), the literal meaning of which is, once again, "change of mind," but which has been routinely butchered in Bible translations as "repentance" by people who did anything but follow Jesus and thus were hardly qualified to translate his words. It is essential to realize that salvation is possible exactly because *we* chose the ego as our teacher and therefore have the power to change our mind. If we do change our mind and choose to follow him, Jesus becomes our teacher, simply because he remembered before we did, not because he is different from us in any other way. In fact, he *is* the demonstration that we would be like him by following him. Jesus in the Course lovingly puts it this way in the closing chapter of the text: "My brother, choose again." (ACIM:T-31.VIII.3:2)

The contorted translation of *"metanoia"* from "change of mind" to "repentance" is completely in line with the dualistic theology which Paul and others gradually developed from their misunderstanding of Jesus and reflects the fact that this became the dominant faction in the tradition. It makes sin real and posits "repentance" as our first step towards becoming Christians. This is the dualistic (if not actually bi-polar!) conversion experience which was Paul's frame of reference. It lets the horse of projection fully out of the barn, not to mention letting it run wild by proselytizing and converting *others*, instead of focusing on changing our own mind, which is what the word *metanoia* originally conveyed. This subtly elevates our existence in this world to the level of "reality" and makes choices in the world important, whereas Jesus was attempting to teach us that sin is not real, because the very thought of separation (the ego) is unreal—it did not really happen. The "change of mind" (the "miracle" of the Course) is the switch from the ego thought system to that of the Holy Spirit. The central tenet of the Course is the Atonement principle, or, once again, the notion that the separation never happened and thus sin is not real. Again, the Course's notion of "Atonement without sacrifice" is based on this idea.

We should realize, however, that the theology that arose

around Jesus—through which Paul and those who followed made an idol out of him and a religion out of his teachings—is simply exemplary of the ego's strategy of co-optation and a subtle substitution of its own thought system for the thought system of the Holy Spirit, which Jesus teaches. They are just the perfect teaching example of all the things we all tend to do to get rid of Jesus, because he is a threat to the thought system which upholds our substitute reality. Again, on a more philosophical level, it could be seen that the belief in a dualistic reality, an existence in the world of time and space, is always an attack on the non-dualistic reality the Course teaches us to be the truth and will inevitably lead us to an experience of separation, conflict, and fear. As the Course states it: "The world was made as an attack on God. It symbolizes fear." (ACIM:W-pII.3.2:1-2) And thus the purpose of our beliefs, which make the world real, is always obfuscation of the truth, namely, the reality of the Oneness of the Kingdom.

For anyone who truly practices what the Course teaches, those moments of recognition will come, when we will see ourselves along the way make all the mistakes which the apostles and Paul made in the Gospel accounts. So those stories have their value, though in a different way from what is commonly understood by Christianity. And today, in the wake of the appearance of *A Course in Miracles*, we see all the same errors being repeated over and over again by various self-proclaimed Course teachers who fundamentally often compromise the non-dualism of the Course by trying to keep some aspect of the world real, thus giving shelter to the ego thought system, which is easily more popular than the stark non-dualism which the Course does teach, if it is properly understood. Gary Renard's work deals with some of those issues in a very clear, yet elegant manner to help keep us Course students on the straight and narrow. I can see already that many people who got confused in the past by some of the teachings that have proliferated around the Course, and managed to miss the point, are now coming back to it after reading Gary Renard's work.

Besides these comments, the most easily available introductory materials on the Course are to be found on the website of the Foundation for *A Course In Miracles*, at www.facim.org, in the Learning Materials section. The Glossary and the summary of Course Theory, which are available there, can be particularly helpful to the newcomer.

As a brief summary of the history of the Course, the main facts are as follows: The book was published in 1975, after it had been channeled through and written down over a period of many years by Dr. Helen Schucman, a research psychologist at the College of Physicians and Surgeons at Columbia University in New York City, in collaboration with William (Bill) Thetford, Ph.D., who was her direct supervisor in their work situation. Her experience was one of a process of inner dictation by a "voice" which she intuitively recognized as that of Jesus, and which is also implied in the text as being his, since he evidently speaks in the first person in the Course.

At the outset, it may have seemed that the Course addressed relationship issues which Helen and Bill were having with each other as well as with colleagues in other departments in their institution (see also Logion 48 in the section "The Logia"), but over time it became clear that the teaching was universal in nature and is addressed to anyone who wants to see how any relationship can be a learning opportunity. Our relationships are thus the best, most natural way to learn to find our way home to inner peace (as opposed to, for instance, secluding oneself in a hermit's cave), if we turn to the Internal Teacher to whom we are led when we follow the instructions from the Course. The form of the Course is a direct address from Jesus to the reader, transmitted in one piece, so that it does not have the history of distortions of the writings from two thousand years ago. Furthermore, no one flunks this course. No Judgments are made, no grades given. No one can *not* pass this course. As the Course itself states it, "...the outcome is as certain as God." (ACIM:T-2.III.3:10)

Following the completion of the Course, a linguistic analysis of the material revealed a sheer masterpiece of literary form, with much of the material written in the form of Shakespearean blank verse. Since it was first published, the Course has become a worldwide phenomenon and is now available in many languages. Its language, however, is not always easy, and Gary Renard's work has become a wonderful introduction for many new students, as well as a refresher for people who are already studying the Course. His work helps the reader to see the Course as a whole and focus on the forest of its overall structure, without getting distracted by the trees. The connection with Thomas, meanwhile, provides the logical linkage to Jesus's original teachings, before Christianity developed its own version out of them.

Closing the Circle:

Pursah's Gospel of Thomas and A Course In Miracles

Text

The core of this book is the text of Pursah's version of the Thomas sayings as our authoritative text and a commentary on them. Because there are so many Thomas translations, the comments about the differences between Pursah's version and the Nag Hammadi tradition are made in a generic fashion under Comments on Form, so the reader may consult whichever edition of the historical text they prefer.

As a practical note, we might mention here that the word "Logion," plural "Logia," has become accepted as the standard Greek designation for direct quotations of Jesus in the original literature to distinguish it from narrative text. "Logion" could be translated as "saying," "word," "quote," "statement," and other similar words, and I have allowed myself some variation in the usage, although when specifically denoting the actual sayings, I have generally used the formal designations of "Logion" and "Logia," in line with this recent tradition.[16]

Comments on Form

The Logia are followed by comments on issues of form, which are concerned with observations on the most salient differences between Pursah's version and the translations of the historical

---

16 This usage is open to question, as documented in *The Critical Edition of Q* (see Bibliography), which (in the introduction by James M. Robinson) makes clear that the more common usage was actually "Logoi," "words," whereas "Logia" has the more formal denotation of "utterances," "pronouncements," etc. The assumption that "Logia" was the standing Greek expression referring to sayings of Jesus may thus go back to a misreading of Papias by Friedrich Schleiermacher in 1832, as argued by Robinson in his introduction. For the purpose of this book, I've chosen to continue this usage which, for the last 150 years, has become the norm.

Coptic text from the Nag Hammadi collection. From this information, we can develop an appreciation of the difficulty of the translation process, and in some cases the edits are a clue to the way in which later embellishments happened in a time when texts were evolving from oral tradition to written text, which was then copied by hand.

Commentaries on Content

Evidently, some of the discussion of the form will directly lend itself to observations about the content. However, this part of the commentary will focus completely on a holistic appreciation of each saying as they appear in the Pursah version, as well as its connection to *A Course in Miracles*.

Needless to say, these commentaries will also ignore any of the sayings which are skipped in the Pursah version because they are at least "suspect," in line with her comments in *Your Immortal Reality*. As a way of highlighting the significance of Pursah's selection, Index 3 offers a comparison of Pursah's selection with the opinion of the Jesus Seminar about their authenticity. The results are quite surprising, including the fact that the Jesus Seminar considers authentic many sayings which Pursah dismisses entirely.

The twenty-two sayings which are included in *The Disappearance of the Universe*, and which in *Your Immortal Reality* are emphatically identified as being "easier to understand" for people of our time, are marked with bold print in the title.

Notes on Pursah's Gospel of Thomas

For the sake of completeness, a brief recap is in order in this place to account for the origin of Pursah's Gospel of Thomas (P/GoTh), though, of course, the interested reader must be referred to *The Disappearance of the Universe* and especially *Your Immortal Reality* to get the first-hand accounts, most particularly Chapter 7 of the latter book. The short version of the story is that Gary meets two ascended masters, who call themselves Pursah and Arten, and who, early on in the conversations recorded in DU, reveal that they were the apostles Thomas and Thaddeus, respectively, in prior incarnations.

An important part of the book is the discussion of twenty-two sayings of the Gospel of Thomas which are identified by Pursah as undoubtedly authentic. Since the entire book can be read as simply a summary of the Course in popular language, the integral discussion of these twenty-two sayings makes a strong case for the continuity between the Jesus of two thousand years ago and Jesus now, i.e., in *A Course in Miracles*. In the same vein, that continuity of thought is available in the lives of all those who do find a relationship with that Internal Teacher through the Course or otherwise.

Index 1 of this book provides a cross reference of P/GoTh to the discussion of the twenty-two sayings that appear in *The Disappearance of the Universe* in order to obviate the necessity of constantly referencing page numbers in the text or using footnotes.

Index 2 provides a cross reference of Thomas Logia to other gospel sources, in particular to the synoptic gospels. Note again the way Pursah highlights—as indicated in the commentaries— that certain Thomas Logia clearly seem to be the original form of sayings we know from the Bible. Intuitively, that historical order makes sense. The cross-index also mentions whether or not certain Logia are co-sourced in Q, the other "sayings" gospel, of which we do not have a written record, but only a reconstruction. It is the tradition which Gary Renard refers to as "The Words of the Master."

Finally, Index 3 correlates the findings of authenticity of the Thomas Logia by the Jesus Seminar (available in the book *The Five Gospels*—see Bibliography) to Pursah's opinion. The differences are noteworthy and hopefully helpful, in particular to the recovering Christians among us who are studying the Course, for it is extremely important to understand that the Jesus of both the Course and the Thomas gospel is completely different from the Pauline version of him which the Christian tradition has handed down to us.

As we allow Jesus to step out of the cloud of historical distortions and listen to what he has to say—as indeed Thomas Jefferson intuitively sensed needed to happen (see Appendix 1)— what comes across is one consistent message, dressed up in different forms according to the time and place where it is being presented. Thus, while it may take us a while to get used to the ancient Middle Eastern imagery of the Thomas sayings, the more we spend time with them, the more they will speak to us and sound increasingly natural, for the message they convey never changes and is always with us. It is the message of God's Answer to the thought of separation, which we thought was an impressive accomplishment, but which the Course refers to as nothing but a "tiny, mad idea" at which we should learn to laugh in order to return home.

Authenticity and Corruption

Furthermore, we should pay attention for a moment to the meta-commentary which Arten and Pursah hand us through Gary in Chapter 7 of *Your Immortal Reality*. Specifically, it is in that chapter where the history of the supposed controversies around the Course, which have raged in recent years, are put to rest. This unfortunate bit of history gives us a tremendous insight into the processes that would cause the corruption of a tradition. Some of the recent disputes and other controversies surrounding the Course seem almost too far-fetched at times, but the process is the same as it always is. We have a polemical literature arguing that the Course does not say what it evidently says, we have polemics over the book itself, and we have alternative versions, some of which were even obtained illegally, and so on. The process is entirely comparable to what went on two thousand years ago, and the upshot is the same: *the world does not want to hear this message.*

Therefore, seeing how the seventy simple sayings Pursah represents as authentic grew into the collection of 114 sayings that was found at Nag Hammadi—which was partially adopted (as quotes in the narrative gospels of the NT) and partially rejected by Christianity—makes it perhaps less surprising that bookshelves have already now been devoted to a variety of interpretations of the Course, which often in one form or another argue that it does not say what it plainly does say. If we understand the tenets of the Course at all, it should be evident that this is merely another demonstration that the world does not appreciate the teachings of Jesus, for the simple reason that he tells us the world is not real, which is one teaching the Course is very emphatic about. It states: "There is no world! This is the central thought the course attempts to teach."(ACIM:W-132.6.2-3) The ego's response seems reasonable enough if your own reality hinges on the notion that the world is real. Consequently, it might be worth noting here that, indeed, without the acceptance or understanding of that central teaching of the unreality of the world, nothing in the Course will make any sense at all.

Then why would anyone study the Course? Because there is a part of our mind that knows Jesus is making sense, and this is what gives us the fortitude to indeed keep seeking until we find. In that process, we begin to recognize our own tendency to make him say what we would like him to say, because that way we only make further detours that delay us on our way. The first requirement of the Course is the "little willingness," which means the willingness to suspect our ego may be wrong and readiness to ask for directions from our Internal Teacher instead. Throughout the Course, Jesus suggests we would save time by following the Course. So his advice boils down to something similar to the rule of Occam's razor or to Socrates's saying that the way you get to the top of mount Olympus is by making sure that your every step goes in that direction. Eventually, we will get tired of the side excursions as we see more and more that a choice for the ego causes us more pain every time. Therein lies the natural limit of our belief in the ego system. As the Course states it: "...you cannot depart entirely from your Creator, Who set the limits on your ability to miscreate." (ACIM:T-2.III.3:3)

The Logia

These are the hidden sayings that the living J spoke and Didymus Thomas recorded:

Logion 1[17]

And he said, "Whoever discovers the interpretation of these sayings will not taste death."

Comments on Form

- There is not much difference here with the translated versions, except:

- Pursah simplifies the name to Didymus Thomas, which means Thomas the Twin.

Logion 1 - Commentary on Content

In the discussion of this saying in *The Disappearance of the Universe*, Pursah says simply, "The word *hidden* means that many of these sayings were spoken by J, either in private or to a very small group of people. It does not mean that it was his intention to hide things." (DU, p. 74) She adds, speaking for herself as Thomas, that this first Logion was actually meant to be an introductory comment by Thomas, not a quote of "J."

We might note that words like "hidden," or "secret," in this present context have played a part in all kinds of mystery cults and secret societies, which made hay out of exactly being secret and playing up that aspect in the form of initiations, which, by and large, degenerated into various fanciful teachings of some kind of secret knowledge that was being imparted to the initiate. This is an evident ego ploy, based on the notion of scarcity, the idea that Jesus somehow would be withholding from us something that we could only obtain at the cost of personal sacrifice. So it is very important to appreciate that this was not Jesus's meaning at all.

Similarly, the very franchise of the Church was based on the notion that there is an exclusive truth, handed down by Jesus to his apostles, the integrity of which was guaranteed by means of the Church's doctrine of "apostolic succession" (see Logion 52, Commentary on Content), the corollary to which is that some people had it and therefore others did not, when his whole point had been that the same mind and the same truth that is in him is in us also. At heart, this whole issue is a typical case of ego projection, for obfuscation is the ego's method for hiding the truth from view, mainly by sending us seeking in the wrong direction (outside) and never finding.

We might also relate this saying to the NT word that Jesus taught in parables, "but to his apostles individually he explained everything" (cf. Mark 4:10 and 4:34), where it is very clear that in his personal relationship with the apostles he does not hold back, even though to the outside world (i.e., the phenomenal world of space and time, duality) he teaches in parables. In other words, to anyone who thinks they are an individual (ego), he speaks in parables, but when we join with him in our mind, we see through the parables and receive direct insight. One of my favorite lines of Ken Wapnick's, which I have heard him say in workshops many a time, is: "The Holy Spirit is a 'what' that looks like a 'who' as long as you think you're a 'who,'" which exemplifies that Jesus is helpful as a symbol for the Holy Spirit as long as we think we ourselves are separate individuals.

We may understand this point as a simple spiritual truth in that, in our relationship with Jesus, the parables of our life are put in a new light and used as a classroom to lead us home, while in the world of time and space everything by definition is metaphor. Finally, it behooves us to seek out that relationship. He will not force us, but he is always present when we ask.

In terms of the Course, the very process of forgiveness reflects this same insight, for taking back our projection and asking Jesus or the Holy Spirit to see things differently induces that teaching moment in which the parables of our life are reinterpreted with Love, and indeed everything is revealed to us in the miracle.

"Will not taste death" means exactly what it says. Our principal confusion with it is that we persistently misinterpret everything he says as being about bodies, since we think we ourselves are bodies, and in our delusion we do not hear that he addresses us as spirit. It just sounds a bit antiquated today, but we can easily get used to that if we imagine ourselves with "J" and his apostles two thousand years ago. Here is the way Pursah addresses this point in *The Disappearance of the Universe*:

> One will not taste death because, as pointed out earlier, J was showing us the way to life—meaning that what we were experiencing here on earth was not life, even though we

assumed it was. He was the living J because he had attained true enlightenment—his oneness with God. *Living*, in this case, does not refer to him being in a body, even though it appeared that he was. It's a reference to the resurrection of the mind, as alluded to earlier—and also referred to a saying from my Gospel that I won't talk about until a later visit. Also, the word *living* here would have nothing to do with a resurrected body, even though J did appear to us after the crucifixion. (DU, p. 74)

This same notion is presented in the Course very clearly in such statements as: "There is no life outside of Heaven. Where God created life, there life must be. In any state apart from Heaven life is illusion. At best it seems like life; at worst, like death." (ACIM:T-23.II.19:1-4)

A nice point also is that, while the "hidden" is prone to a paranoid ego misinterpretation, the "Whoever discovers" seems to make clear that the door is open to whoever wants to bother with the truth. The implication of such teaching is the same as that of *A Course in Miracles*, namely, that salvation is a choice on our part, not a thing that is bestowed on us selectively and passively. And the relationship with our Internal Teacher is one we have to consciously seek out and develop, a process in which the Course provides guidance. Our seeking should be deliberately under-taken; we do not discover the meaning of these teachings by accident, but only because we enter a relationship with our Internal Teacher and learn to make the choice for truth, as we learn to see that it is dearer to us than the lies of the ego.

We end up realizing that there is no *terra incognita* "out there" waiting to be discovered; the "unknown" in the world outside (projected from our mind) is merely the corollary of declaring our identification with the ego as the "known," which leaves all else as the unknown, an always threatening world, which maintains its status, courtesy of our refusal to know our true Self as spirit, in the Mind of God. That also is what was meant by the inscription "Know Thyself" (Gr. *gnothi seauton*) in the forecourt of the Temple of Apollo at Delphi. In the Course, Jesus invites us to take that journey with his love beside us to shine away the fear that protects the ego thought system in our mind. Related to this is the Course's notion that the experience of the failure of prayer stems from the fact that our will is not unified: as long as we still entertain the ego (fear), we maintain a split mind, and it is forgiveness which enables us to heal the split one step at a time.

Logion 2

J said, "Those who seek should not stop seeking until they find. When they find, they will be disturbed. When they are disturbed, they will marvel, and they will reign over all."

Logion 2 – Comments on Form

- Obviously, the main difference between the Nag Hammadi-based versions and the Pursah version is the choice of the word "disturbed." Some translations use "troubled," which could easily be a translation problem, though I cannot judge the original Coptic word. The translation of the Jesus Seminar makes the same choice as that of the Meyer translation.

- The authority of Pursah's version (should you choose to accept it) lies mainly in making these difficult translation choices, because she represents that this is how it sounded originally; and, who knows, perhaps some scholar will one day follow her suggestion and develop an Aramaic version of the Pursah kernel.

Logion 2 – Commentary on Content

The "seeking," which cannot fail to result in finding, is the seeking for the origin of the "tiny, mad idea," the ego's detour into fear (the returning from the Omega back to the Alpha), which can only be undone by choosing "another way" (see Logion 48) in the eternal "now," where the choice between ego and Holy Spirit is forever open to us.[18] When we do find our way back to that point, we will reign over all, for it is then that we can change our mind and let the air out of the balloon of the ego thought system, which is what the title of *The Disappearance of the Universe* alludes to and what the Course calls "accepting the Atonement for ourselves," our only true function here (e.g., ACIM:T-14.IV.3:6-7).

It needs no comment that this is highly disturbing to us, as long as we identify ourselves with the ego thought system. This word per se could be understood on several levels, but perhaps what is the most relevant is to realize that the attraction we feel for the ego rests on the fact that we made it up and we believe we are it, so that we fear that making the other choice means the end of us. What it would mean, in fact, is the ending of our identification with pain and suffering, crucifixion and death, and a resurfacing in the stream of Life instead, for it is the illusory life of the separated self which is death.

This saying is also familiar to us from the Sermon on the Mount as recorded in Matthew and Luke, and it seems to go back to both the Thomas and the Q traditions, so Thomas in this case is not the unique source. The form in Matthew 7:7 is: "Seek and you will find; knock and the door will be opened to you." [King James Version (KJV)] Another parallel passage is Luke 11:9-10.

---

18 Cf. ACIM-T.27.VIII.6:2-5: Into eternity, where all is one, there crept a tiny, mad idea, at which the Son of God remembered not to laugh. In his forgetting did the thought become a serious idea, and possible of both accomplishment and real effects. Together, we can laugh them both away, and understand that time cannot intrude upon eternity. It is a joke to think that time can come to circumvent eternity, which *means* there is no time.

On one level, the notion of "seek and you will find" seems to instill the same idea as the Course's "The secret of salvation is but this: that you are doing this unto yourself." (ACIM:T-27.VIII.10:1) and other similar messages, not to mention the overall idea that "This is a course in mind training." (ACIM:T-1.VII.4:1), all of which seek to wake us up to the fact that we do have a mind and the capacity to change our mind and choose "another way." Salvation is thus a choice, a result of deliberate seeking, not a matter of fate and passively "being chosen," as this word has been misunderstood to mean in the Christian context, where the emphasis is shifted more and more to our sinfulness, and the notion that we have a mind that needs to choose is obliterated. Christianity is fundamentally based on an endorsement of the ego's littleness, which makes us "sinners all."

We should also remember that the Course teaches that the purpose of the body is to make us mindless, to play the victim and be merely an effect of the world. In waking up to the mind, we are taking responsibility for our lives, realizing that our mind is the cause, and until such time, we are powerless to change anything. Changing something in the world becomes uninteresting once we realize it is an illusion. What we change is our allegiance to the illusion itself.

As to the "reigning over all," there are countless ways that the Course makes clear to us that we are giving up our power by choosing the littleness of the ego, whereby we, in effect, choose slavery over freedom. The main principle underlying this expression is that the cause of anything is always in the mind, so that is where our power lies, while in the world we are literally powerless and at the effect of the world, and our most impressive actions amount to nothing more than rearranging the deck chairs on the Titanic. One relevant quote is:

Few appreciate the real power of the mind, and no one remains fully aware of it all the time. However, if you hope to spare yourself from fear there are some things you must realize, and realize fully. The mind is very powerful, and never loses its creative force. It never sleeps. Every instant it is creating. It is hard to recognize that thought and belief combine into a power surge that can literally move mountains. It appears at first glance that to believe such power about yourself is arrogant, but that is not the real reason you do not believe it. You prefer to believe that your thoughts cannot exert real influence because you are actually afraid of them. This may allay awareness of the guilt, but at the cost of perceiving the mind as impotent. If you believe that what you think is ineffectual you may cease to be afraid of it, but you are hardly likely to respect it. There *are* no idle thoughts. All thinking produces form at some level. (ACIM:T-2.VI.9:3-14)

Logion 3

J said, "If your teachers say to you, 'Look, God's Divine Rule is in the sky,' then the birds will precede you. If they say to you, 'It's in the sea,' then the fish will precede you. Rather, God's Divine Rule is within you and you are everywhere. When you know yourself, you will be known, and you will understand that we are one. But if you don't know yourself, you live in poverty, and you are the poverty."

Logion 3 – Comments on Form

• The translations from the Nag Hammadi text tend to speak of "leaders" in lieu of "teachers." Clearly, Pursah is suggesting that the original word sounded different from these translations of it—from Coptic to English, and from Greek to Coptic before that. It is easy to imagine this difference of word choice as a typical translation problem of choosing the right word. In this case, "leaders" is a very ego-bound word since leaders have "followers," and this usage looks at us as sheep who need to be led, which is just one more variation on the ego's victor/victim psychology. On the other hand, "teacher" versus "students" keeps the emphasis on our capacity to learn and our responsibility for learning. "Leaders" fits more with the Christian model, and "teachers" fits more with the Course model. The Course usage makes it very clear that the right-minded teacher will truly see it as his mission to bring the student to equal himself in learning, and that thus the difference between teacher and student is only a difference in time, and time is itself unreal.

- "God's Divine Rule" as a modern English equivalent of "the Kingdom of Heaven" is interesting, and, for one thing, it may bypass the association with the Messiah/King, which was certainly one of the "bitter idols" (ACIM:C-5.5:7) the world made of Jesus. We should notice that the same crowds (us = ego!) who shouted "Hosannah" hollered "Crucify him!" with equal ease once the expected King of the Jews disappointed them as a defenseless wimp. Most helpfully, the expression "God's Divine Rule" has perhaps a more abstract quality to it. It is at least noteworthy that Pursah here elects to differ in usage with both the Course and the Bible for obviously very deliberate reasons: at the very least, she wants us to think again about an all-too-familiar term. Her word choice here is similar to those of the translations of the Jesus Seminar.

- The phrase "is within you and you are everywhere" seems to focus on the fact that, as in the Course, Jesus speaks to us as spirit, as Sons of God who know who they are. Thus, versions like "is inside you and it is outside of you" (Meyer et al.) seem to be spoken to bodies, whereas the Pursah version addresses the Son of God as spirit, in a similar vein as the Course does throughout.

- Likewise, the phrase "that we are one" is a more forceful and direct expression than "you are children of the living Father" (or similar words) in the Nag Hammadi-based versions. The former emphasizes the oneness of the Sonship, again, as spirit, whereas the latter is a lovely reflection of our dependence on our Father but lets stand the illusion that we are individuals (i.e., "children" in the plural).

Logion 3 – Commentary on Content

The comment about the birds and the fish are to me a reminder of the statement in the Course that our path to God is "a journey without distance to a goal that has never changed" (ACIM:T-8.VI.9:7), as well as to the Course's clarification that the ego's motto is: "Seek but do not find." (ACIM:W-71.4:2) Whenever we think that the Kingdom, or God's Divine Rule, is elsewhere, and is somewhere we have yet to get to (and this is invariably what the ego would have us believe), that is merely a new disguise for reaffirming the separation all over again, for it is nothing but the thought that we could ever be outside of God's Divine Rule.

There are no magical saviors in the world outside of us, there is no place to get to, and the only journey is the removal of the blocks to "the awareness of love's presence" (ACIM:Introduction), which we ourselves have erected and have to dismantle on the way back home. This is a beautiful image to remind us of the fact that there is nothing but our own fear that keeps us from remembering that God's Divine Rule is within, which is right here, right now, and it never was otherwise to begin with. We are one with all we know.

For the rest, the last line is rather interesting, and I think it could be paraphrased as follows: "If you know who you are as the Son of God, others will recognize that in you, and you will live in the abundance of the spirit." Compare this to the Course's statement: "You do not change appearance, though you smile more frequently. Your forehead is serene; your eyes are quiet. And the ones who walk the world as you do recognize their own." (ACIM:W-155.1:2-4) If you do not know who you are (i.e., by believing you are an ego), then you live in lack (of the Love of God), i.e., in the ego's thought system of scarcity, obviously by virtue of the fact that we ourselves chose the separation, not because God would be withholding it from us.

One final observation is that it should be quite obvious why Thomas was expurgated from the "canonical" tradition, as this statement completely contradicts the eschatological notions that Paul, c.s., built into the emerging "Christian" theology, where the Kingdom is relegated to the future, along with the Second Coming (in bodily form), which completely obfuscates the notion of joining with Jesus in the Second Coming right now by finally opening the door to him (in our hearts) instead of slamming it shut. Therefore the saying "do this in remembrance of me" in Luke 22:19 was intended by Jesus to be about joining with him in our mind in the present, not magically (and cannibalistically) sharing his body in the hope he might come back someday in the future. (See ACIM:T-7.V.10.) In other words, the point is that Jesus is present to us in our mind any time we remember him. We do not have to wait for him to come to us; he is waiting for us to come to him. The Pauline position is the ego's ploy of putting him off into the future and accusing him of not coming back when he promised.

Logion 4

J said: "The person old in days should not hesitate to ask a little child the meaning of life, and that person will live. For many of the first will be last, and they will become a single one."

Logion 4 - Comments on Form

- The Pursah version drops the "seven days old," the words used in the various translations to describe the "little child," which would seem to be a somewhat superfluous literary exaggeration and evidently a later addition.

- Some of the translations have "place of life" instead of "meaning of life," which seems odd, but it may technically be an appropriate translation of the Coptic. Clearly, the purpose of Pursah's revisions is to be closer to how it really sounded to a listener in those days.

Logion 4 – Commentary on Content

This statement reminds us of the Course's frequent image that, as adults who think they are all grown up because we are supposed to be able to judge for ourselves, we are really spiritual children, not to mention children who live in the hell of separation. In that context, the Jesus of the Course holds himself out as our "elder brother" (cf. ACIM:T-1.II.3:7) who can guide us on the way home.

It also alludes to the Alpha and Omega or, as the Course might put it, the return to the moment of the decision, where we can make another choice. So if we ask one who is not burdened by years of ego conditioning—a "little child" (an allusion to the growing of the Christ-child within us)—about the meaning of life, we can learn to make the other choice (the "other way"—see Logion 48, Commentary on Content). The image here is that the Christ-child within us is the little spark of light, that memory of Heaven which may seem ever so faint when we first become aware of it, but grows ever stronger as we begin to pay attention and listen. The Christophorus legend[19] reflects this same notion.

The phrase "the first will be last" takes a different form here from that in the versions we find in the Synoptics, where it is followed with "and the last shall be first," so that, at first blush, the statement might seem to carry the biblical image "first out of

---

19 The Christophorus legend has it that a strong man, named Reprobus, asked a Christian monk how best to serve Jesus, whereupon he was directed to carry people across a dangerous river at a ford. One day, a little child showed up. Reprobus picked him up, but, as he carried him across, the child became heavier and heavier. When they reached the other side, Reprobus asked him who he was. The child revealed that he was Jesus and proceeded to baptize him in the river, changing his name to Christophorus, i.e., "Christ carrier." In a Christian editing of the legend, the weight is explained by the fact that Jesus presumably carries the sins of the world. A deeper truth is suggested by Dutch author J.W. Kaiser (see Bibliography), namely, that on the spiritual journey we seem to feel more and more burdened by what Jesus asks of us (we think we are carrying him) along our journey (which is also the point of the book *The Dark Night of the Soul* by St. John of the Cross), until we realize that the only burden was the ego's resistance and that, in the world into which Jesus leads us (across the river), all is light and abundance. Jesus in fact has been carrying *us* all along.

the gate" versus "last to come home." However, seen in the context of the Course, the notion that "when we do come back to the decision-making point, we will remember our oneness" is strongly reinforced here (the first *is* the last). Furthermore, the "first" in this context seems to have the quality of "The ego always speaks first [and is always wrong]." (Cf. ACIM:T-6.IV.1:2.) The outcome—the Atonement—is inevitable.

Logion 5

Know what is in front of your face, and what is hidden from you will be disclosed to you. For there is nothing hidden that will not be revealed.

Logion 5 - Comments on Form

- Regarding this saying, there is total agreement between the Nag Hammadi versions and Pursah's, except, of course, for minor word choices of translators.

Logion 5 – Commentary on Content

In *The Disappearance of the Universe*, Pursah comments as follows (connecting from the discussion of saying 23): "In order to win, however, you must—as saying number 5 puts it: [text of saying 5 follows]. What is in front of your face is illusion, and God's Kingdom—which appears to be hidden—will be revealed to those who learn from the Holy Spirit the unique way of forgiving whatever is in front of them the way J did. Eventually you will be one with him, and there will be nothing left but your true joy in the Kingdom of Heaven." (DU, p. 77) A very comprehensive statement of this same idea can be found in the Course's section "What is a Miracle?" (ACIM:W.pII.13)

In a form different from that in Logion 1, we can see in this statement an antidote to the ego's tendency to act as if Jesus were hiding something from us. This misunderstanding was later exploited in various cults and secret societies by teachers seeking power and authority over their followers, as opposed to Jesus, who offers empowerment and restoration of our true Will.

It is also very much a reflection of a Course teaching with which we are now very familiar: what we deny we must project. Conversely, as Ken Wapnick described it in an article, we should see "The World As The Royal Road To Heaven." (*The Lighthouse* newsletter, Vol. 7, No. 2, Foundation for *A Course in Miracles*, June 1996)

The implication is that if we really pay attention to what is in front of us, the ego's hidden motives will become visible to us and can be forgiven. This is a very simple and straightforward expression of the thought process for practicing the Course's fundamental teaching of forgiveness (see Logion 58), which inevitably reveals the Kingdom to us.

Logion 6 (14)

The disciples asked him, "Do you want us to fast? How should we pray? Should we give to charity? What diet should we observe?" J said, "When you go into any region and walk in the countryside, and people take you in, eat what they serve you. After all, what goes into your mouth will not defile you; rather, it's what comes out of your mouth that will reveal you."

Logion 6 - Comments on Form

- Pursah's editing seems to address a very obvious correction, which, from a standpoint of scriptural scholarship, could only be guessed at but not seriously entertained without sources to support such a version. The result of her edit here is a very straightforward and convincingly clear question and answer, thanks to the removal of some material that at least in part seems out of context, even if it might otherwise seem legitimate on text-critical grounds. The material from Logion 6 falls in that category. The material removed in saying 14 would, at first blush, very likely seem suspect and out of character, so its removal intuitively makes sense.

- Note that Pursah also provides an explicit comment on the issue of the confluence of these two Logia, saying in *Your Immortal Reality:* "...because they got mixed up over the years, but parts of them contain a true saying." (YIR, p. 161)

Logion 6 – Commentary on Content

Pursah's contracted version makes for a straightforward instruction by "J," encouraging us to let go of the ego's emphasis on form over content, and instead to honor only content and adapt to whatever form seems appropriate at the time. We should concern ourselves with the question of whether we are channeling either the ego or the Holy Spirit, for only what we say will reflect whom we have chosen as our teacher. The circumstances and the form are irrelevant.

This statement also reminds us of an instruction from the Course, "...you need do nothing." (ACIM:T-18.VII.5:5), the antidote to the ego's always wanting to "do" something on the level of form. Lastly, the following quote from the Course also connects to the present saying, reflecting the same truth that "what comes out of your mouth" will be telling:

> There is a way of living in the world that is not here, although it seems to be. You do not change appearance, though you smile more frequently. Your forehead is serene; your eyes are quiet. And the ones who walk the world as you do recognize their own. Yet those who have not yet perceived the way will recognize you also, and believe that you are like them, as you were before. (ACIM:W-155.1)

Logion 8

J said, "A wise fisherman cast his net into the sea. When he drew it up it was full of little fish. Among them he discovered a large, fine fish. He threw all the little fish back into the sea, and he chose the large fish. Anyone here with two good ears should listen."

Logion 8 - Comments on Form

- Compared to the Nag Hammadi version, the Pursah version makes this saying more direct by leaving out some words.

Logion 8 – Commentary on Content

The statement reminds us of the words that we find in the Synoptics where "J" tells the apostles (his Course students *avant la lettre*) to follow him and he will teach them to become fishers of men. Also, the story of the loaves and the fishes come to mind, another NT parable regarding the unlimited, infinite nature and abundance of spiritual nourishment, as opposed to the crumbs that the world offers.

Thus, in the forms we find in that great river of life, there are many who speak to us of the ego's scarcity and one ("J") who speaks to us of the abundance of spirit, and clearly, if we are wise, we should choose that one.

Again, we may note that the typical mistake in subsequent tradition has been to apply statements that concern the spirit to the level of the world, something the Course calls "level confusion" (in Chapter 2 of the Text). This ego-obfuscation has obliterated the meaning of Jesus's sayings in later tradition. The currently popular obsession with "abundance" in that sense is thus revealed as a crypto-Calvinistic concept, and it is not at all what Jesus means in any of these statements, since he invariably addresses us as spirit, what we are in reality. After all, even in the NT, we see Jesus's teachings about "level confusion" in such passages as Matthew 16:11, where he says: "How is it ye do not understand that I spake it not to you concerning bread,..." (KJV), and so then, as now, he teaches in parables to a world of duality, but to his disciples individually he explains everything. We only have to come to him; he will not force us, for he will not preempt the power of our mind.

Logion 9

J said, "Look, the sower went out, took a handful of seeds, and scattered them. Some fell on the road, and the birds came and ate them. Others fell on the rocks, and they didn't take root and didn't produce grain. Others fell on the thorns, and they choked the seed and the worms ate them. And others fell on good soil, and it produced a good crop; it yielded sixty per measure and one hundred twenty per measure."

Logion 9 - Comments on Form

- Pursah's edits here appear rather minor and of the cosmetic variety.

Logion 9 – Commentary on Content

This is, of course, in other variants, a well-known parable, and it provides yet another image to express the idea that the seeds of our newfound spirituality, which Jesus sows liberally, do not grow well in the ego's soil. But when we start following Jesus and provide the seed with the right soil, it will yield results beyond all measure of what our puny ego-expectations could ever comprehend. This is how we also learn the Course's lesson, "I am under no laws but God's." (ACIM:W-76)

To emphasize once more the Course's perspective on the traditional image of following Jesus in his footsteps, we realize more and more that we are traveling a path that he took first, and that the specifics (form) of our path are different from his life circumstance but the *content* is the same as that which he demonstrated to us. This is why he also says, "I do not call for martyrs but for teachers." (ACIM:T-6.I.16:3), which is the correction to the mistaken notion that *imitatio Christi* was about copying the form, specifically his suffering and death, when it was intended to be about learning the content, which was the love. In the same chapter, he also emphasizes that the mission is to "Teach only love, for that is what you are." (ACIM:T-6.III.2:4) This is the difference between following him with the ego or with the Holy Spirit as our teacher.

Logion 11

The dead are not alive, and the living will not die.

Logion 11 - Comments on Form

Here we have a case of fairly radical surgery, though in a very straightforward fashion. The accretions, which Pursah's scalpel cuts away in part at least, have a bit of a (later) gnostic smell to them, and what is left is clean and straightforward.

Logion 11 – Commentary on Content

The very brief Jesus quote we are left with parallels the Course's "There is no life outside of Heaven." (ACIM:T-23.II.19:1)

The result of Pursah's edits is straightforward and forceful, one of the typical "level one" statements which are designed to confront us with the Reality that *is*, as opposed to the pseudo-life, the ego's illusory dream-world, which the Course refers to as existence. The ego's dream is a dream of death.

It is important to understand the distinction, both here and in the Course, that the sayings come in the language of metaphor but speak on the level of spirit, so we need to listen with our heart, lest we misinterpret them and throw them out as worthless and contradictory, as Christianity did.

Logion 13

J said to the disciples, "Compare me to something and tell me what I'm like." Simon Peter said to him, "You are like a just angel." Matthew said to him, "You are like a wisdom teacher." Thomas said to him, "Master, my mouth is utterly unable to say what you are like."

And he took him, and withdrew, and spoke three sayings to him. When Thomas came back to his friends, they asked him, "What did J say to you?"

Thomas said to them, "If I tell you one of the sayings he spoke to me, you will pick up rocks and stone me, and fire will come from the rocks and consume you."

Logion 13 - Comments on Form

- Pursah makes some minor word choices that sharpen the language a bit.

- One puzzling line from the Nag Hammadi texts that appears to be contradictory is eliminated, and the result is a much more coherent and relevant statement.

Logion 13 – Commentary on Content

This saying would be a big question mark, were it not for the material that has already been provided in *The Disappearance of the Universe*, where Pursah reports the three things Jesus said to her that day, i.e., during her previous incarnation as Thomas:

> You dream of a desert, where mirages are your rulers and tormentors, yet these images come from you.
> Father did not make the desert, and your home is still with Him.
> To return, forgive your brother, for only then do you forgive yourself.
>
> (DU, p. 81)

These lines make complete sense in the context of *A Course in Miracles*, being the modern elaboration of Jesus's teachings. The notion that this world is a desert (which we must leave) is a central tenet of the Course, and the notion of forgiveness (in forgiving our brother we are forgiving ourselves) is the central teaching of the Course. In *The Disappearance of the Universe* (pp. 81-82), Pursah uses Logion 13 to introduce Gary to *A Course in Miracles*.

With the Course, we would also note that the title "Master" is not meant to elicit awe, but rather respect, as one would have for an elder brother. And the most common-sense reason for calling Jesus "Teacher," or "Master," is that he speaks with an authority that is completely alien to the ego—the certainty of spirit versus the uncertainty of the ego—which as students we lack unless and until we ourselves become fully identified with the thought system of the Holy Spirit. That shift of perception—the miracle—is all about the difference between Knowledge and perception, another important contrasting pair of level-one and level-two concepts in the Course,

Knowledge being of spirit, level one, and perception being of the ego and the world of separation, or level two.

The reference to the stoning and the fire that consumes are, of course, allusions to the ego's fear of the imaginary wrath of God, which is the archetypical projection of the ego's thought system, which serves to defend itself against our looking at it with Jesus's vision, as it cannot stand the light. As long as we are suitably afraid of looking, the ego thought system is assured of our allegiance. It is when we start to look at the ego in the light of Jesus's vision that it shifts "from suspiciousness to viciousness," as the Course speaks of it in Chapter 9 (ACIM:T-9.VII.3:7), because the darkness of the ego is afraid the light would shine it away.

Logion 17

J said, "I will give you what no eye has seen, what no ear has heard, what no hand has touched, and what has not arisen in the human heart."

Logion 17 - Comments on Form

- Word choices aside, there is perfect agreement here between the Nag Hammadi versions and Pursah's version.

Logion 17 – Commentary on Content

This saying reminds me of the Course's statements about the Real World, i.e., once we do accept the Atonement for ourselves, and therein take Jesus as our guide permanently, we will see the world through his vision, and we will see a forgiven world, very different from the projected world of hatred, which the ego has shown us.

Here is one passage that speaks of this shift in the context of our relationships in the world:

> Across the bridge it is so different! For a time the body is still seen, but not exclusively, as it is seen here. The little spark that holds the Great Rays within it is also visible, and this spark cannot be limited long to littleness. Once you have crossed the bridge, the value of the body is so diminished in your sight that you will see no need at all to magnify it. For you will realize that the only value the body has is to enable you to bring your brothers to the bridge with you, and to be released together there.

> The bridge itself is nothing more than a transition in the perspective of reality. On this side, everything you see is grossly distorted and completely out of perspective. What is little and insignificant is magnified, and what is strong and powerful cut down to littleness. In the transition there is a period of confusion, in which a sense of actual disorientation may occur. But fear it not, for it means only that you have been willing to let go your hold on the distorted frame of reference that seemed to hold your world together. This frame of reference is built around the special relationship. Without this illusion there could be no meaning you would still seek here. (ACIM:T-16.VI.6-7)

Another aspect of this statement is the notion that reality is not at all impacted by our temporary illusion of separation, the ego and the world. As the Course so beautifully puts it: "...not one note in Heaven's song was missed." (ACIM:T-26.V.5:4)

Logion 18

The followers said to J, "Tell us how our end will be."
He said, "Have you discovered the beginning, then, so
that you are seeking the end? For where the
beginning is, the end will be. Fortunate is the one who
stands at the beginning: That one will know the end
and will not taste death."

Logion 18 - Comments on Form

- Word choices aside, there is agreement with Nag Hammadi,
  except for Pursah's convention of "J" in lieu of Jesus.

Logion 18 – Commentary on Content

This statement ties in with references to the Alpha and the Omega with which we are familiar from other Thomas sayings (Logia 2, 4, and 106) and the book of Revelation. In terms of the Course, what comes to mind is the notion that accepting the Atonement means to return to the moment of decision when we chose the ego and to choose the Holy Spirit instead. When we come back to the decision moment, having tasted the ego's hell, we can see right through that story to the end, and we then make the other choice.

It is a mistake to think that this sort of terminology makes Jesus a gnostic. Rather, the gnostics simply retained and developed certain ideas of Jesus which may have been lost—if not actively suppressed—in other traditions.

Another Course parallel comes to mind as well: "The world is not left by death but by truth, and truth can be known by all those for whom the Kingdom was created, and for whom it waits." (ACIM:T-3.VII.6:11)

Logion 20

The disciples said to J, "Tell us what God's Divine Rule is like." He said to them, "It's like a mustard seed. It's the smallest of all seeds, but when it falls on prepared soil, it produces a large plant and becomes a shelter for birds of the sky."

Logion 20 - Comments on Form

- Here again we have agreement of the versions, except for the convention of "J" versus Jesus, and minor word choices, depending on which translation you consult.

Logion 20 – Commentary on Content

This is a famous quote, for one because it recurs in the canonical Gospels. It speaks to us (in the form of a parable, as usual) of the unimaginable abundance of the order of spirit. Many related expressions could be found in the Course, starting with: "Those who witness for me are expressing, through their miracles, that they have abandoned the belief in deprivation in favor of the abundance they have learned belongs to them." (ACIM:T-1.IV.4:8)

Logion 22

When you make the two into one, and when you make the inner like the outer and the outer like the inner, and the upper like the lower, and when you make male and female into a single one, so the male will not be male and the female will not be female...then you will enter the Kingdom.

Logion 22 - Comments on Form

- Pursah edits out some sections entirely. And what she dismisses is illustrative of how the sayings might have been embellished and framed in stories after the fact.

- We note that, in this instance, Pursah uses the traditional translation "Kingdom" and does not attempt to use, with the Jesus Seminar, the phrase "God's Divine Rule." Also of interest is Pursah's capitalization of Kingdom, which would seem to emphasize that this is no ordinary kingdom, but a Kingdom not of this world. The Course commonly uses the term "Kingdom" and, in the same spirit as that of Pursah, capitalizes the word when referring to the Kingdom of Heaven.

Logion 22 – Commentary on Content

The content of the statement is very clear, simple, and straight-forward, but, if you think duality is reality, it would seem the height of confusion and obfuscation. The point simply is that if we practice forgiveness and heal the separation, i.e., if we accept the Atonement for ourselves, then all differences will fall away, because we give up our belief in them as we rejoin the Kingdom. The manifestation of dualism in every instance is merely an expression of our choice for the separation, and so choosing the Holy Spirit, in lieu of the separation thought (the ego), means the healing of duality at every level and the restoration of oneness.

As always, we should not take this statement too literally, for while we are in the body, those apparent distinctions will continue to be with us, although they will cease to be important, as we no longer depend on them for our sense of identity. In short, when our attention shifts to content, the apparent differences of form lose meaning.

Logion 23

I shall choose you, one from a thousand and two from ten thousand, and they shall stand as a single one.

Logion 23 - Comments on Form

- Variations in word choices aside, there is no material difference here between Pursah's version and the Nag Hammadi translations.

Logion 23 – Commentary on Content

Here is what Pursah has to offer in *The Disappearance of the Universe*:

> Of course, J chooses everyone, all the time. But how many are ready to listen? As this saying obviously foretold, the lessons of the Holy Spirit will not be listened to by the masses. But the ones who listen, who *are* the chosen ones, will surely stand as a single one—for that is what they are. God's Son shall return to the Kingdom whole and complete, and in the end there will be no one who does not stand with us. The J underground cannot lose. (DU, p. 77)

There is hardly anything to be added to the above commentary, except perhaps the obvious point that it evidently connects well to the following Course passage:

> "Many are called but few are chosen" should be, "All are called but few choose to listen." Therefore, they do not choose right. The "chosen ones" are merely those who choose right sooner. Right minds can do this now, and they will find rest unto their souls. God knows you only in peace, and this *is* your reality. (ACIM:T-3.IV.7:12-16)

And finally, once we accept the Atonement for ourselves, and thus heal the separation within ourselves, we will know experientially that we are one with all our brothers in the Sonship. In other words, we certainly will stand as a single one, for there really is only one Son.

Logion 24

The disciples said, "Show us the place where you are, for we must seek it." He said to them, "Anyone here with two ears had better listen! There is a light within a person of light, and it shines on the whole world. If it does not shine, it is dark."

Logion 24 - Comments on Form

- Pursah's version here has only trivial cosmetic changes.

Logion 24 – Commentary on Content

This statement is pretty straightforward, and it can be linked to numerous passages in the Course which express that, in choosing forgiveness, the love and the light are extended through us. A related notion, that "it is as blessed to give as to receive," as stated in the sixteenth Miracle Principle (ACIM:T-1.I.16), gives similar expression to the need for the awareness of flow through us, so we can be a channel (cf. ACIM:W-rV.in.9:2-3, as well as Logion 26, Commentary on Content). This image connects smoothly to the Course's idea that it is our job to remove the "blocks to the awareness of love's presence" (Introduction).

One of the persistent themes evidently is, once again, the notion that seeking outside is a doomed ego enterprise and the way of the spirit is to seek inside. The statement's notion "there is a light within a person of light" might also remind us that these Jesus Logia, too, have for their purpose what the Course describes as its only purpose: "...to provide a way in which some people will be able to find their own Internal Teacher." (Preface, "How It Came" section) No external teacher will ever be able to help us if we do not first commit to the light within.

Logion 26

You see the speck that is in your brother's eye, but you do not see the log that is in your own eye. When you take the log out of your own eye, then you will see clearly enough to take the speck out of your brother's eye.

Logion 26 - Comments on Form

- The differences here are only minor word choices. Pursah chooses "log" in lieu of the traditional "beam."

Logion 26 – Commentary on Content

The Disappearance of the Universe (p. 79) combines the discussion of Logia 26, 31, 36, and 54 by pointing out that some of the Thomas sayings were very closely quoted in the canonical literature of the NT and were, in Pursah's words, "prequels" (see Index 2). What matters is the impression that the Thomas version of such sayings has the feel of being the most primitive, most original, and least polished compared to the Gospels of the NT Canon. This idea would have to occur to any attentive reader, and it has led a growing body of biblical scholars to consider that the internal evidence places Thomas clearly before the canonical Gospels, and therefore, more importantly, before the editorial influence of Paul. Understanding this temporal sequence makes it clear why the Jesus of Thomas does not sound at all like a Christian, and this observation has caused some consternation among those who come from a Christian background but find themselves accepting the authenticity of the Thomas document nevertheless. In fact, not only should any attentive reader notice this issue, but we should note that when Jefferson sat down those few evenings (see Appendix 2) to cut and paste what was to become the "Jefferson Bible," he astutely discerned the same editorializing influence of Paul and rigorously edited those sections out. Quite remarkably, he did this long before the rediscovery of the Thomas gospel, prior even to the discovery of the Oxyrhynchus fragments.

Any form of "helping" which the ego comes up with pursuant to its crooked so-called vision is always an attack, for it involves projection of our own guilt onto our brother. And only when we accept the Atonement for ourselves—i.e., fully and experientially realize that nothing ever happened and the "tiny, mad idea" (the separation) was just a momentary illusion and a silly mistake— can we be helpful to our brothers. In other words: physician heal thyself. The Course makes it clear that the healing can flow through us only if we accept it for ourselves first.

This is also why the Course says: "The sole responsibility of God's teacher is to accept the Atonement for himself." (ACIM:M-18.4:5), but it (along with Logion 24) also emphasizes the flow of healing through us as we get our ego out of the way, as in the following:

> For this alone I need; that you will hear the words I speak, and give them to the world. You are my voice, my eyes, my feet, my hands through which I save the world. The Self from which I call to you is but your own. To Him we go together. Take your brother's hand, for this is not a way we walk alone. In him I walk with you, and you with me. Our Father wills His Son be one with Him. What lives but must not then be one with you? (ACIM:W.rV.in.9:2-9)

Throughout the Course, the logic is that we can only be helpful to our brother by accepting the help for ourselves first and extending it. If we attempt to help with the ego, we always cause festering wounds.

Logion 28

I stood in the world and found them all drunk, and I did not find any of them thirsty. They came into the world empty, and they seek to leave the world empty. But meanwhile they are drunk. When they shake off their wine, they will open their eyes.

Logion 28 - Comments on Form

- There are some simplifications in the first sentence compared to the Nag Hammadi translations. Omitted is a sub-sentence which, indeed, rings more like a statement edited by a scribe than like the original statement.

- Importantly, there is the "they will open their eyes" in lieu of what some render in typical Christian fashion as "they will repent." This is a most interesting edit, for it makes Jesus sound like Jesus rather than Paul. The whole evolution of the meaning of the Greek word "*metanoia*" from "changing your mind" to "repentance" represents the transition from Jesus to Paul, and from Jesus's teachings to the doctrines of Christianity.

Logion 28 – Commentary on Content

This Logion is a very straightforward picture of how, as sons of the ego and under its spell, we are all drunk with the values of the world and have no time for Jesus and his precepts. In that condition, we are destined to leave the world (in death) as empty as we came, with our guilt unhealed and therefore doomed to repeat the same mistakes *ad infinitum*. This is hell right here, right now; it has nothing to do with an afterlife.

And indeed, the ego's ideas of "living on purpose" and a "fulfilling" life are designed to keep Jesus safely outdoors—while we remain sound asleep, having supposedly a better dream. Unless and until we shake off our allegiance to the ego system, we will not open our eyes—something that begins with our looking for "another way." (See Logion 48.)

Another common-sense way of understanding this saying is that, as long as we are convinced that our life is working well just as it is, there is no motivation to be looking for *any* other way.

Logion 31

A prophet is not acceptable in his own town. A doctor does not heal those who know him.

Logion 31 - Comments on Form

- There are only cosmetic changes.

- Note the more direct style Pursah uses here, leaving off the "Jesus said," resulting in cleaner rendering of the statement.

Logion 31 – Commentary on Content

In *The Disappearance of the Universe,* Pursah offers little comment on this statement and a few others she considers NT "prequels." (See Index 2.) She observes that they are quoted in the canonical Gospels, warns against overly literal interpretations, and alerts us to the fact that their meaning is often different from what we might have received from the Christian tradition.

That comment perhaps touches on the essence of this statement, the main point being that we should not let our perceptions be based on the past, but rather learn to hear things fresh, now. Stereotypes do prevent us from seeing what is right in front of our eyes. And so, if we think on the level of the world that we know someone and yet that person is offering us a miracle, we are likely to reject it when we react to that person based on the past in ego terms (our so-called "experience"), instead of actually hearing what they are offering us in the here and now. So our pat judgment and closed-mindedness will block healing opportunities. This is a familiar theme from the Course, where, in such sections as "Cause and Effect" (ACIM:T-1.2.VII), Jesus makes it clear that he will only come in at our invitation.

Every encounter is, of course, a "holy encounter" (ACIM:T-8.III.4:1) in the making, as we always meet a Holy Son of God, an epiphany which the ego seeks to prevent by ensuring that we see the person in terms of his or her past and therefore as a body.

Logion 32

J said, "A city built on a high hill and fortified cannot fall, nor can it be hidden."

Logion 32 - Comments on Form

- Pursah offers no significant deviation here from the historical text.

Logion 32 – Commentary on Content

This saying introduces a new theme thus far, which is reminiscent of the Course's notion that the ego system is "...fool-proof, but it is not God-proof." (Cf. ACIM:T-5.VI.10:6.) In other words, the ego's thought system, for all its apparent logic, rests on a faulty premise and is therefore ultimately shaky. Truth, on the other hand, is true and rests on a firm foundation (the proverbial rock, here: a "high hill"), and while truth is evidently solid, in essence it is hidden in plain sight. There is no room for doubt if you really give it an honest look.

Logion 34

J said, "If a blind person leads a blind person, both of them will fall into a hole."

Logion 34 - Comments on Form

- Pursah offers no changes here.

Logion 34 – Commentary on Content

While this is a pretty familiar saying, it can be understood in a great many ways and has often been used as such with great effect. The fundamental teaching has mostly been lost amidst the smart-ass applications of this sort of "Duh!!!" statement—which it seems to be, if misquoted in just the right way.

The real point of the teaching is, of course, that if my brother and I are listening to the ego, we are knee-deep in dreck, and the counter to that predicament from the Course would be reflected in the quote:

Whoever is saner at the time the threat is perceived should remember how deep is his indebtedness to the other and how much gratitude is due him, and be glad that he can pay his debt by bringing happiness to both. Let him remember this, and say:

I desire this holy instant for myself, that I may share it with my brother, whom I love.
It is not possible that I can have it without him, or he without me.
Yet it is wholly possible for us to share it now.
And so I choose this instant as the one to offer to the Holy Spirit, that His blessing may descend on us, and keep us both in peace.

(ACIM:T-18.V.7)

We see here how, both in the Thomas quote and in *A Course in Miracles*, there is a subtle focus on learning within the context of our relationships. In other words, to use the words of the Logion, if one of these two blind people realizes his blindness and turns to the light of the Holy Spirit, which provides the Answer (cf. ACIM:T-27.IV.7:5), we find the miracle instead of another problem coming out of the ego's horn of plenty (plenty of problems, that is), with which it wants to keep us engaged in making meaningless changes in the world as a way to distract us from our power to change our mind.

Logion 36

Do not worry, from morning to night and from night until morning, about what you will wear. The lilies neither toil nor spin.

Logion 36 - Comments on Form

* Pursah streamlines this statement, but also adds the last sentence, with which we are familiar from part of another very similar quote found in the gospels of Luke (12:27-28) and Matthew (6:28b-30) and also in Q.

Logion 36 – Commentary on Content

It is clear that Pursah's treatment does not add anything structural to this saying, but she simplifies it and makes it more rounded and more quotable. On p. 79 of *The Disappearance of the Universe*, she emphasizes that this saying is not meant in a physical sense, but concerns itself with our mental attachments.

The underlying thought is akin to the Course's "I need do nothing." (cf. ACIM:T-18.VII:passim) and Gary's comment, "The Holy Spirit doesn't do form." (DU, p. 287) As such, it is the counter to the ego's endless concern with specifics, with form, with externalities, which forever serve only one purpose: to keep us completely enmeshed in the ego thought system and "blissfully" (with tongue firmly in cheek) unaware of who we are as spirit. To the ego system, only form provides a firm foundation; to spirit, form is merely the effect and temporary in nature. The Course's section on the "Development of Trust" addresses our transition "to the stage of real peace." (ACIM:M-4.I.A)

Logion 37

When you take your clothes off without guilt, and you put them under your feet like little children and trample them, then you will see the son of the living one and you will not be afraid.

Logion 37 - Comments on Form

- Apart from some minor edits, the most notable change is Pursah's elimination of an introductory sentence, a lead-in question from the followers, apparently because it is a later editorial adulteration. The net effect of the change is that the statement now sounds as though it is addressed to the reader, thereby becoming that much more direct.

Logion 37 – Commentary on Content

Jesus is hardly advocating nudism here. Rather, this statement addresses the ego's obfuscations and teaches that we should discover the innocence underneath the appearance. It is a corollary to the Course's "...defenses *do* what they would defend." (ACIM:T-17.IV.7:1) and an equivalent of "In my defenselessness my safety lies." (ACIM:W-153:passim) Our defenses are the ego's clothing, which only serves to hide the ego's self-accusation that we have sinned, and our realization that we do not need those defenses anymore is big step forward. This idea is based on understanding experientially that under the "clothing" of our "adult" defenses is an innocent child of God. Our defenses choke the child half to death, and this Logion invites us to let the defenses go and set the child free. Growing up, in worldly terms, does entail building up defenses; growing up spiritually means letting them go.

We could collect a lengthy list of the words the Course uses to point out to us the ego's ways of hiding from sight what it is up to and the importance of catching on and seeing through its antics. One line that comes to mind in this context is: "Be very honest with yourself in this, for we must hide nothing from each other." (ACIM:T-4.III.8:2) There, Jesus encourages us in effect to open ourselves up to him and let his light shine in on the murky darkness of the ego, which must yield to the light always. This Logion is yet one more way of expressing this idea.

Logion 40

A grapevine has been planted outside of the Father, but since it is not strong, it will be pulled up by its roots and shall pass away.

Logion 40 - Comments on Form

- Pursah's rendering omits the "Jesus said" lead-in and has somewhat smoother wording.

- No substantial changes otherwise.

Logion 40 – Commentary on Content

This is an evident parallel to the Course statement that the ego thought system of separation (vine planted outside of the Father) is not viable, because it is based on an "insane premise," as the Course refers to it in the following passage:

> The authority problem is still the only source of conflict, because the ego was made out of the wish of God's Son to father Him. The ego, then, is nothing more than a delusional system in which you made your own father. Make no mistake about this. It sounds insane when it is stated with perfect honesty, but the ego never looks on what it does with perfect honesty. Yet that is its insane premise, which is carefully hidden in the dark cornerstone of its thought system. And either the ego, which you made, *is* your father, or its whole thought system will not stand. (ACIM:T-11.in.2:3-8)

On p. 149 of *The Disappearance of the Universe*, Pursah emphasizes, in connection with this statement and Logion 56 as well, the notion that the nature of this world is that of a dream and not reality. In other words, the insane premise is the ego, and all the imaginations flowing out from that one original "tiny, mad idea" are unreal.

The Course alludes to this issue in several ways, but the following paragraph is just as foundational as the one quoted above:

> Yet in this cloud bank it is easy to see a whole world rising. A solid mountain range, a lake, a city, all rise in your imagination, and from the clouds the messengers of your perception return to you, assuring you that it is there. Figures stand out and move about, actions seem real, and forms appear and shift from loveliness to the grotesque. And back and forth they go,

as long as you would play the game of children's make-believe. Yet however long you play it, and regardless of how much imagination you bring to it, you do not confuse it with the world below, nor seek to make it real. (ACIM:T-18.IX.7)

Logion 41

J said, "Whoever has something in hand will be given more, and whoever has nothing will be deprived of even the little they have."

Logion 41 - Comments on Form

- The Pursah rendering offers no variations worthy of note.

Logion 41 – Commentary on Content

The path home runs contrary to the ego's valuations, regardless of what they are. This transition process is described throughout the Course, most specifically and systematically in the "Development of Trust" section. (ACIM:M-4.I.A.3-8) The ego wants Jesus to be Santa Claus, always giving us what we think we want, but the Holy Spirit gives us what we need in truth, not what we want and merely imagine we need.

Logion 42

Be passersby.

Logion 42 - Comments on Form

- Pursah strips it down to the statement only, omitting "Jesus said."

Logion 42 – Commentary on Content

When Pursah introduces this quote in *The Disappearance of the Universe*, she emphasizes that this also has nothing to do with the physical realm and with giving anything up. It evidently pertains to our mental attachments that we need to let go of, by stopping to take things so personally.

In accordance with the Course, we note that this is another way of saying that we need to watch our thoughts. (See, for example, ACIM:W-44.7.) To the extent that we can learn to be in the observer role, we can dissociate from our identification with the ego and join with Jesus, instead of blindly acting out in the world.

Logion 45

Grapes are not harvested from thorn trees, nor are figs gathered from thistles.

Logion 45 - Comments on Form

- Oh what a relief it is to have Pursah around to decisively rid us of the editorial extensions to this statement! They were troublesome to say the least, and this definitive edit is helpful indeed.

- As a side note, we might realize that Pursah's edits here highlight the process of historical distortions which increasingly crept into the simple teaching of Jesus, as it evolved in the popular stories and was written down in the novellas we now know as the "canonical" Gospels, as the Church self-servingly labeled the books, which reflected *its* version of Jesus.

Logion 45 – Commentary on Content

With these edits, we now have the opportunity to reflect on the original statement. The way it strikes me immediately is that it is a warning along the lines we very much know from the Course, that the choice is between love and fear and that the ego can never bear fruit. There is no hope in waiting until the dream gets better. It will not. The only course of action is not to choose the ego, but to choose the Holy Spirit's thought system of Love instead, and that is where the fruits are. What also comes to mind is the comment Jesus once made to Helen Schucman: "The thing to do with a desert is to *leave*." (As reported in Ken Wapnick's *Absence from Felicity*, p. 236.)

Logion 47

A person cannot mount two horses or bend two bows. And a servant cannot serve two masters, or that servant will honor the one and offend the other. Nobody drinks aged wine and immediately wants to drink young wine. Young wine is not poured into old wineskins, or they might break, and aged wine is not poured into new wineskins, or it might spoil. An old patch is not sewn onto a new garment, since it would create a tear.

Logion 47 - Comments on Form

- Pursah offers no material changes, except the direct form, without the "J(esus) said."

Logion 47 – Commentary on Content

Here is how Pursah prefaces this statement in *The Disappearance of the Universe*:

Today, you and your friends believe in the existence of a trilogy—body, mind, and spirit. The "balance" of all three is important in your philosophy. But you will soon learn instead that the seemingly separated mind, which makes and uses bodies, must choose *between* the changeless and eternal reality of spirit—which *is* God and His Kingdom—or the unreal and ever-changing universe of bodies—which includes *anything* that can be perceived, whether you appear to be in a body or not. This is a cornerstone of J's message. He really did say, as it was recorded by me in what is now labeled saying number 47. [Text of Logion 47 follows, and conversation is picked up by Gary.]

GARY: Are you saying that giving equal value to body, mind, and spirit actually *contributes* to me coming back here over and over again as a body, rather than being free?

PURSAH: Yes, but this doesn't mean that you should neglect your body. We're speaking of another way of looking at it. To finish the point about my past beliefs, my Gospel merely recorded things J had said. Unlike the writers of the later Gospels, I was not constantly inserting my opinion. Thus, *Thomas* is not so much a reflection of my level of understanding at that time as it is a record of some of J's ideas....

(DU, p. 76)

This statement reflects the many ways in which the Course reminds us that our one real choice is all or nothing, love or murder, and no compromise is possible. Accepting the Atonement means realizing that nothing happened, and thus the ego and the world are utterly meaningless and non-existent, as stated, for example, in the following quote:

> Life and death, light and darkness, knowledge and perception, are irreconcilable. To believe that they can be reconciled is to believe that God and His Son can *not*. (ACIM:T-3.VII.6:6)

One could hardly think of a more explicit way of saying it, and the only reason we read right over it, and do not hear what it says, is fear, because we still believe we are protected by our belief in the ego. In *The Disappearance of the Universe* (p. 76), Pursah connects this statement direct to Logion 61.

Logion 48

J said: "If two make peace with each other in a single house, they will say to the mountain, 'Move over here!' and it will move."

Logion 48 - Comments on Form

- Pursah makes no material changes, except the "J" instead of "Jesus."

Logion 48 – Commentary on Content

The holiest of all the spots on earth is where an ancient hatred has become a present love. And They come quickly to the living temple, where a home for Them has been set up. There is no place in Heaven holier. And They have come to dwell within the temple offered Them, to be Their resting place as well as yours. What hatred has released to love becomes the brightest light in Heaven's radiance. And all the lights in Heaven brighter grow, in gratitude for what has been restored. (ACIM:T-26.IX.6)

This Logion clearly expresses the Course's idea of the miracle as the choice in the mind for the solution ("the Answer") instead of the problem ("the question"), which changes everything.

The story of the origin and scribing of the Course itself is also a reflection of this statement, in that Helen Schucman and William Thetford clearly made a deliberate choice to find a way out of the endless professional rivalries at their place of work and seek "another way." The answer turned out to be the "other way" given them by Jesus in the Course, which speaks of the other way of perceiving (the miracle). I do not know which would be more difficult—moving a mountain or producing the Course—but, without a lot of help, it would be an insurmountable task, and that is the point here. (See also the section "On The Course" in this book.)

Logion 49

Fortunate are those who are alone and chosen, for you will find the Kingdom. For you have come from it, and you will return there again.

Logion 49 - Comments on Form

- Pursah drops the "Jesus said."

- No other differences other than variations in word choices in different translations.

Logion 49 – Commentary on Content

In her comment on p. 80 of *The Disappearance of the Universe*, Pursah points out the parallel between this Logion and the parable of the prodigal son and emphasizes that we will return home again. She comments further, "In this saying, such people are alone because they know that there is really only *one* of us. Of course they are not really alone, because they have the Holy Spirit." (DU, p. 150)

I hear an allusion to the biblical word that to his disciples individually, Jesus explains "everything," which is entirely in line with a major theme of the Course, which says, "Its only purpose is to provide a way in which some people will be able to find their own Internal Teacher." (ACIM:Preface) The Course emphasizes throughout that it is necessary to ask Jesus into our life, i.e., to join with him in our mind, that is, with that part of the mind which still knows the Sonship is one. Also, we need to be alone in the sense of not being preoccupied with the special (external) relationships the world holds out to distract us and literally tempts us to divert our attention from the inner space where Jesus awaits, beckoning us to follow him out of the world.

The second part of this statement conveys the same notion that the Course refers to as "a journey without distance to a goal that has never changed." (ACIM:T-8.VI.9:7), or "There is no life outside of Heaven." (ACIM:T-23.II.19:1) Also, repeated references like "...the outcome is as certain as God." (ACIM:T-2.III.3:10), not to mention "You are at home in God, dreaming of exile..." (ACIM:T-10.I.2:1), all paraphrase the same notion in different ways, namely, that the Atonement merely means the waking up to the fact that nothing ever happened and all the hoopla in between was just a dream.

Logion 51

The disciples said to him, "When will the rest for the dead take place, and when will the new world come?" He said to them, "What you are looking forward to has come, but you don't know it."

Logion 51 - Comments on Form

• Pursah's edits offer minor cosmetic changes only.

Logion 51 – Commentary on Content

This statement also connects very strongly to several passages in the Course, starting perhaps with the notion that our journey is already over and that our only problem is that we keep choosing to relive that ancient "moment of terror" (see, for example, ACIM:T-27.VII.13.3) when we conceived the notion of the separation from oneness. The Course is here to help us learn to stop making that very self-defeating choice, so that what remains is what already is, always was, and always will be: "We say 'God is,' and then we cease to speak, for in that knowledge words are meaningless." (ACIM:W-169.5:4)

The following passage may make this even clearer:

Time really, then, goes backward to an instant so ancient that it is beyond all memory, and past even the possibility of remembering. Yet because it is an instant that is relived again and again and still again, it seems to be now. And thus it is that pupil and teacher seem to come together in the present, finding each other as if they had not met before. The pupil comes at the right time to the right place. This is inevitable, because he made the right choice in that ancient instant which he now relives. So has the teacher, too, made an inevitable choice out of an ancient past. God's Will in everything but seems to take time in the working-out. What could delay the power of eternity? (ACIM:M-2.4)

We might also note that it is statements like this one which would run afoul of the then-emerging orthodoxy, in which Jesus was being misinterpreted more and more as a figure in the world of time and space and "the Second Coming" as a future event in which he would come back for us and for which we had to prepare. This is the typical upside-down logic of the ego, which always proposes solving the problem by first making it good and real and then bringing the solution to the problem, while Jesus in the Course gives us the practical advice of bringing the problem ("the question") to the solution ("the answer"), so that the former simply disappears. (Cf. ACIM:T-27:IV.7:5.)

Logion 52

The disciples said to him, "Twenty-four prophets have spoken in Israel, and they all spoke of you." He said to them, "You have disregarded the living one who is in your presence, and have spoken of the dead."

Logion 52 - Comments on Form

- Pursah here chooses the more traditional "disciples" instead of the more general "followers." In Course terms, one might think of "students."

- Note also that, at the time the Thomas sayings were recorded, the stylistic "Twelve" of the canonical Gospels, which is symbolic of all of us (the twelve being the signs of the zodiac), is not yet in place as a fixed cast of characters in a quasi-mythological way, so the term "disciples" still would have a more generic meaning.

Logion 52 – Commentary on Content

To the ego, eternity just seems to be "a lot of time," and since it lives in the past, longevity is how it measures relevance and authority, since it cannot see what is in front of our eyes for what it is. We might note that this makes no sense on many levels. Even mathematically it is clear that "infinity" is a limit, which can never be reached—within the ego system, we might add.

This statement is very interesting as a rebuke to the ego's need to look to the past for an explanation of time, which is "blasphemy" to what we are as spirit. The ego is always afraid in the presence of the immediacy of spirit, uses the past to defend itself and its values, and thus avoids surrendering to the immediacy of the spiritual present.

In a way, this statement is an anticipatory refutation of the Church's doctrine of "apostolic succession," which is an obviously false construct on which Christianity sought to found the substitute authority of the Church. The upshot of it is that Jesus is very much brought down into this world, in which authority rests on physical relationships, tradition, and longevity in terms of time and space. The notion of "apostolic succession" starts with the self-serving and retroactive myth that Peter was the first Pope and that Jesus's teachings were somehow passed on through the lineage of successive popes. Hence: the great importance of the ritualistic selection of the next Pope. This notion is as silly and irrelevant as the "bloodline of Christ," which is receiving a lot of attention lately by people who believe Jesus and Mary Magdalene had children, who carried on their work. The idea was given currency by the book *The Da Vinci Code* and many other sources, though it is unclear to me what it rests on. In both cases, formalities and physical realities are given precedence over spirit, which is the opposite of what Jesus would teach, as when he said, "For whosoever shall do the will of God, the same is my brother, and my sister and my mother." (Mark 3:35, KJV) In other words, Jesus believes in content, not form, yet the world wants to legitimize its bastardization of his teaching by a formal justification such as "apostolic succession," which is clearly equally as irrelevant as the notion of being a blood relative.

In this world, we all make this same mistake all the time. We think granite is solid and mud is not, forgetting that these differences are just part of the illusion, the purpose of which is to delude us into thinking that anything here should be eternal. Thus we are "tempted" to put our stock in the world of time and space and bring Jesus down into the world to fix it for us, instead of realizing that our eternal reality (or should I say our "Immortal Reality?") is only in Heaven with God and that what we should do is follow him *out* of this world. Somehow, the notion of "apostolic succession" presumes to bear down on us with the authority of two thousand years of unbroken tradition in this world, where nothing is permanent.

With regard to the Course, we see the same thing happening again. For example, there are those who even try to give the Course a false historical authority by calling it the third testament. And there is plenty of confusion about the Jesus of the Course, who is *not* the Jesus of Christianity, for the same reasons as this Logion, too, reflects.

In contrast to the NT Gospels, the interesting thing about the Thomas/ACIM connection is that, first, in Thomas, we hear only Jesus's *teachings* and *not* the historical narratives and mythologies that built up around him during the decades following his death, nor are we subjected to Paul, c.s., who rendered the religion that was named after Jesus suitable for service to Caesar (the world, the ego). Similar to Thomas, the Course delivers the direct literal and unedited words of Jesus *today* without historical distortions and misunderstandings, politicizing, textual corruption, and translation errors. If you want to know what Jesus says, just go to the book, and there it is. No research or translation necessary, and the form is that of a direct address to the reader.

Finally, on yet another level, this statement is a wonderful reminder of just how foolish and misguided the search for the historical Jesus is, when the problem is that we are not listening to him today! As a typical example, the book *The Five Gospels* has the subtitle "What Did Jesus Really Say?" and these words on the cover: "The Search for the Authentic Words of Jesus." We may presently be able to appreciate why such concerns are an ego-diversion, when the object is to listen to Jesus in our own life today.

Logion 54

Fortunate are the poor, for yours is the Father's Kingdom.

Logion 54 - Comments on Form

- Pursah drops the "Jesus said," as per usual.

- The Pursah version is also more direct about whose Kingdom we're talking about—not just any old kingdom, but "the Father's."

Logion 54 – Commentary on Content

It has been a perennial favorite in Christianity to distort statements along these lines by taking them literally, which traditionally has helped to make Christianity popular as a state religion, serving as it did to keep impoverished citizens in good spirits by promising a better life in Heaven, in a distant future. On p. 79 of *The Disappearance of the Universe,* Pursah again specifically warns against taking this statement literally. Clearly, it speaks of *mental* attachments, not attachments to *things.* She clarifies this idea further with the important point that if we believe we have to give something up, we are making it just as real as when we covet it.

We could contrast this with the following saying in the Course: "Forget this world, forget this course, and come with wholly empty hands unto your God." (ACIM:W-189.7:5) Clearly, the drift is that everything of form, including the Course itself, is to be taken figuratively, not literally, and it only serves to tide us over, to help us make the journey, and then its utility is over and we should let go of *all* our investments in the world of form. The time involved in our experience corresponds to our resistance to laying down our ego-defenses against the truth, for the path in truth is, once again, "a journey without distance to a goal that has never changed." (ACIM:T-8.VI.9:7) "Poor," in that sense, means free of attachments to the ego-world of scarcity and lack, so that we have our hands free to accept the abundance of spirit, which our true home in Heaven offers us.

Logion 56

Whoever has come to understand this world has found merely a corpse, and whoever has discovered the corpse, of that one the world is no longer worthy.

Logion 56 - Comments on Form

- As per usual, Pursah thinks the "Jesus said" speaks for itself, since this is a "sayings" gospel.

- For the rest, the Pursah version makes some word choices that make it flow a little better than the Nag Hammadi translations.

Logion 56 – Commentary on Content

One significant difference with the Nag Hammadi versions is that Pursah studiously avoids the word "know" in connection to the world, evidently because of its special meaning of the word in Course terms and in the tradition, as expressed originally in the concept of "gnosis." This ties in closely with her comments relating to this statement and Logion 40 as well (see there). To use the word "understanding" is a bit lighter, though in terms of the Course this word goes beyond the superficial intellectual grasping to an inner, experiential understanding, which certainly leads us towards a true "knowing."

For the rest, this statement is entirely in line with the Course's notion that "The world was made as an attack on God." (ACIM:W-pII.3.2:1) and represents the crucifixion, as well as the notion that "What is not love is murder." (ACIM:T-23.IV.1:10) In a somewhat tongue-in-cheek way, Jesus wryly observes that the world is no longer worthy of us (cf. Logia 80, 85, and 111, commentaries on content), since we now know it to be nothing, and so, naturally, we learn to see it for what it is. This same notion—of the world not being worthy of us—is taken up in the Course here:

Whenever you question your value, say:

God Himself is incomplete without me.

Remember this when the ego speaks, and you will not hear it. The truth about you is so lofty that nothing unworthy of God is worthy of you. Choose, then, what you want in these terms, and accept nothing that you would not offer to God as wholly fitting for Him. You do not want anything else. Return your part to Him, and He will give you all of Himself in exchange for the return of what belongs to Him and renders Him complete.

(ACIM:T-9:VII.8)

Logion 57

God's Divine Rule is like a person who had good seed. His rival came during the night and sowed weeds among the good seed. The person did not let the workers pull up the weeds, but said to them, "No, otherwise you might go to pull up the weeds and pull up the wheat along with them. For on the day of the harvest the weeds will be conspicuous, and will be pulled up and burned."

Logion 57 - Comments on Form

- Here again Pursah prefers "God's Divine Rule" in lieu of the phrase "the Father's Kingdom," which is interesting, inasmuch as "Kingdom" in this sense is quite commonly used in the Course, but evidently she feels this phraseology has some merit.

- She also chooses "rival" in lieu of the more common "enemy," which seems to be more general.

- Finally, she clarifies "them" as "the workers."

Logion 57 – Commentary on Content

This image seems very reminiscent of the Course's notion that resisting "evil" serves to make it real and reinforces the ego thought of separation, and therefore forgiveness is the only path that makes any sense. Anything we do to "take care of the problem" accomplishes the opposite, namely, it makes the problem real. And in forgiveness everything gets washed away, and the ego will "fade into the nothingness from which it came..." (ACIM:M-13.1:2).

In short, as the Course has it, "defenses *do* what they would defend." (ACIM:T-17.IV.7:1), so resisting the world "makes the problem real," while choosing the miracle, and letting the light of the Holy Spirit shine away the darkness of the ego, merely dispels our illusions without effort.

Logion 58

J said, "Congratulations to the person who has forgiven and has found life."

Logion 58 - Comments on Form

- Pursah offers some very salient differences here, as compared to the various historical-text translators who, in lieu of the term "forgiveness," allude to "working hard" (Meyer), or "have undergone ordeals" (Leloup), the latter of which seems overly interpretative and Christian in tone in that it connotes that suffering and sacrifice is somehow part of "purification," which is nothing Jesus ever taught.

Logion 58 – Commentary on Content

Clearly, persisting in our forgiveness work is the farewell to the ego thought system of death, and as we unlearn our stubborn habit of choosing the crucifixion and death, we realize there really is only one choice that is real, and it is life.

There are any number of passages in the Course which clarify the black-and-white nature of the choice to be made. One of them is:

> You who believe that God is fear made but one substitution. It has taken many forms, because it was the substitution of illusion for truth; of fragmentation for wholeness. It has become so splintered and subdivided and divided again, over and over, that it is now almost impossible to perceive it once was one, and still is what it was. That one error, which brought truth to illusion, infinity to time, and life to death, was all you ever made. Your whole world rests upon it. Everything you see reflects it, and every special relationship that you have ever made is part of it. (ACIM:T-18.I.4:1-6)

With reference to the comment on form above, while clearly Pursah's word choice indicating what the work *is* instead of just referring to "hard work" is clearer than that of *inter alia* Meyer and Leloup, we should note that forgiveness surely is hard work at times. Also noteworthy is the fact that forgiveness in the context of the Course ("forgiving" our brother for what he has *not* done, forgiving ourselves for what we have *not* accomplished [separating from God], and recognizing that all which seems to occur in front of us is, in fact, literally being projected from the mind) is the work that is explicitly meant here. In the context of the Course, the reason it is such hard work is because of our own tremendous resistance against accepting responsibility for the decision of separation; yet our only hope of changing that decision lies in recognizing that very thing: our resistance to it. Without that realization, we would be powerless victims of the world. Every ounce of ego in us resists this notion of being responsible for the decision, simply because the thought itself comes unglued when we get to that realization.

Logion 59

Look to the living One as long as you live. Otherwise, when you die and then try to see the living One, you will be unable to see.

Logion 59 - Comments on Form

• Here Pursah offers only minor variations compared to the translations.

Logion 59 – Commentary on Content

"Its only purpose is to provide a way in which some people will be able to find their own Internal Teacher." This is what the Course says about itself in the Preface, and clearly throughout the book a central focus remains on having us develop a solid relationship with this Internal Teacher, whom we in the West most commonly refer to as Jesus, but who could be J, Krishna, Buddha, Quan Yin, God's Help, or whatever name is symbolic to you of that eternal Love, which says: indeed everything is alright, and all is forgiven. We may also note that this statement is absolutely opposite to Christian theology, which puts the Second Coming off into the future and makes it into an event in the world that (but of course) never comes, for that is the ego's favorite song: "Tomorrow, tomorrow, tomorrow, tomorrow." And thus Jesus can safely be postponed, while we continue the ego's racket.

This saying could not state more clearly that the very purpose of putting Jesus off is to ensure we shut ourselves out from his love, which is the essence of the ego's choice for the separation. Again, no wonder the nascent Church could not get along with the Thomas gospel, as the belief spread that we were waiting for him to come back to us in the world, when all the while he was waiting for us—then as now—to follow him *out* of this world and to make the choice for life now, rather than to postpone it to a time beyond the grave. In other words, decide to follow Jesus now, and do not put off until tomorrow what you can do today. That is the message.

Logion 61

I am the one who comes from what is whole. I was given from the things of my Father. Therefore, I say that if one is whole, one will be filled with light, but if one is divided, one will be filled with darkness.

Logion 61 - Comments on Form

- Pursah goes to work with a carving knife here, instead of the more usual scalpel, and she eliminates fully two thirds of the text, which has grown to be a little story, reminiscent of the style of the canonical Gospels. She restores just the core of Jesus's saying.

Logion 61 – Commentary on Content

In *The Disappearance of the Universe,* Pursah connects this statement direct to Logion 47, and she comments,

> In other words, to revisit an earlier point, you can't have it both ways. You can't be a little bit whole, any more than a woman can be a little bit pregnant. Your allegiance must be undivided. You must be vigilant only for God. This state of mind does not come all at once; it takes a lot of practice. (DU pp. 76 ff.)

This statement sounds very much like the Course. It also contains an allusion to the NT parable of the prodigal son, which Arten and Pursah clearly regard as authentic (DU p. 9 ff.). In fact, the Course itself quotes it (cf. ACIM:T-8.VI.4), making clear that the choice between the ego and the Holy Spirit is either/or, black or white. And of the two thought systems, only one is true: the one that reflects wholeness, our right mind, and the home of the Holy Spirit.

Logion 62

J said, "I disclose my mysteries to those who are ready for my mysteries. Do not let your left hand know what your right hand is doing."

Logion 62 - Comments on Form

- Pursah picks the usual "J" for "Jesus."

- Most translations use other terms for Pursah's "ready," so this word choice seems to be her unique contribution.

Logion 62 – Commentary on Content

This statement sounds close to a point Ken Wapnick has often raised in workshops, namely, that for the purposes of the Course we have just one hand, and if we give Jesus that hand, we are not giving it to the ego. In other words, the two thought systems— that of the ego and that of the Holy Spirit—are mutually exclusive. (See, for example, ACIM:T-6.V.C.4.7, as well as Logion 66, Commentary on Content.) So, do not check back, for the ego will always hinder you by wanting to bring baggage along. Just trust the process and go.

Or, to use a contemporary idiom as an analogy: when we want to listen to the Holy Spirit, the ego will invariably offer: "On the other hand...," and then give us all the reasons not to listen to that still, small voice within.

Logion 63

There was a rich person who had a great deal of money. He said, "I shall invest my money so that I may sow, reap, plant, and fill my storehouses with produce, that I may lack nothing." These were the things he was thinking in his heart, but that very night he died.

Logion 63 - Comments on Form

- Interestingly, Pursah leaves off the "ears to hear" quote, which we find in the Nag Hammadi versions. Obviously, "J" sometimes used that expression, but here Pursah dismisses it.

Logion 63 – Commentary on Content

Obviously, when we invest with the ego in permanence in the world, in resistance against the spontaneity of spirit, we die. Right then and there. For it is the choice for death. This is why the Course says the world was made as an attack on God. Our investment in the things of the world is our defense against God. We either choose the ego or the Holy Spirit, and only one of them is real—and it is not the ego (which *is* death).

To put it another way, scarcity is an ego-belief resulting simply from the choice for the separation, and it is not solved with knowing things about the world, but only by accepting the Atonement for oneself, which is the Course's word for the realization that the separation never occurred and which represents the choice for life.

Logion 66

J said, "Show me the stone that the builders rejected. That is the keystone."

Logion 66 - Comments on Form

- The Pursah version offers minor differences.

- She chooses "keystone" instead of "cornerstone," which most translations use.

Logion 66 – Commentary on Content

The ego always speaks first and is always wrong.

This is reminiscent of the Course's Workbook lesson, "I am under no laws but God's." (ACIM:W-76), as well as statements from the text such as: "There is nothing in the world to teach him that the logic of the world is totally insane and leads to nothing. Yet in him who made this insane logic there is One Who knows it leads to nothing, for He knows everything." (ACIM:T-14.I.3:8-9)

Which is to say that our understanding of the situation is not at all relevant; neither is our "logic," for it is always based on the ego's selective substitute reality. But Jesus, or the Holy Spirit, sees the whole and can correctly identify the keystone in the situation. This imagery is also interestingly similar to the familiar statement from the canonical tradition that "not one stone shall remain on the other." (Mark 13:2)

In another parallel to the Course, the notion that, once again, the thought systems of the ego and the Holy Spirit are altogether mutually exclusive (see, for example, ACIM:T-6.V.C.4.7, as well as Logion 62, Commentary on Content.) is also very pertinent here, and this is certainly a colorfully illustrative way to express just that.

Logion 67

J said, "Those who know all, but are lacking in themselves, are completely lacking."

Logion 67 - Comments on Form

- Pursah makes some fairly superficial changes, mostly the plural versus singular, which makes the statement more general.

Logion 67 – Commentary on Content

This statement clearly refers to the typical ego-concept of knowledge—knowing "things" about the world outside of us—as opposed to the inner knowing of the nature of things. That kind of knowledge is the typical "temptation" which the ego holds out to us as a worthwhile objective because it keeps us "seeking and not finding." (See, for example, ACIM:T-16.V.6.5.) Looking outside of ourselves is the ego's attempt to satisfy the insatiable hunger resulting from the thought of scarcity. And so, when we fill ourselves with that kind of knowledge, it cannot fill the gaping hole within.

Logion 70

J said, "If you bring forth what is within you, what you have will save you. If you do not have that within you, what you do not have within you will kill you."

Logion 70 - Comments on Form

• Pursah offers no changes here.

Logion 70 – Commentary on Content

This saying is an interesting corollary to such Course notions as "giving and receiving are the same" (see, for example, ACIM:T-25.IX.10.6); i.e., in the experience of the miracle, we receive love ourselves by choosing to extend it to our brothers. It is through this experience that Jesus, or the Holy Spirit, teaches us who and what we are in truth.

If we hang on to the ego thought system of scarcity and lack instead of that abundance of the spirit, we are indeed choosing death, and that kills us. The Course says: "Who with the Love of God upholding him could find the choice of miracles or murder hard to make?" (ACIM:T-23.IV.9:8)

Logion 72

A person said to him, "Tell my brothers to divide my father's possessions with me." He said to the person, "Brother, who made me a divider?" He turned to his disciples and said to them, "I'm not a divider, am I?"

Logion 72 - Comments on Form

- The one salient change here is from "Mister," or "Man," in the translated versions, which sounds kind of denigrating, to "Brother," which sounds more true to form.

Logion 72 – Commentary on Content

The statement is a perfect parallel to the Course's teachings that the ego's way of giving is a win/lose proposition, "giving to get," whereas the Holy Spirit's way of giving (of love) is always win/win.

The following passage demonstrates the point, and there are many others:

> The higher mind thinks according to the laws spirit obeys, and therefore honors only the laws of God. To spirit getting is meaningless and giving is all. Having everything, spirit holds everything by giving it, and thus creates as the Father created. While this kind of thinking is totally alien to having things, even to the lower mind it is quite comprehensible in connection with ideas. If you share a physical possession, you do divide its ownership. If you share an idea, however, you do not lessen it. All of it is still yours although all of it has been given away. Further, if the one to whom you give it accepts it as his, he reinforces it in your mind and thus increases it. If you can accept the concept that the world is one of ideas, the whole belief in the false association the ego makes between giving and losing is gone.
>
> Let us start our process of reawakening with just a few simple concepts:
>
> *Thoughts increase by being given away.*
> *The more who believe in them the stronger they become.*
> *Everything is an idea.*
> *How, then, can giving and losing be associated?*
>
> (ACIM:T-5.I.1:6-2:5)

We may note that this Logion is also an implicit allusion to wholeness of spirit. Dividing anything is not the work of Jesus or the Holy Spirit; wholeness and healing is.

Logion 75

J said, "There are many standing at the door, but those who are alone will enter the bridal suite."

Logion 75 - Comments on Form

- No change, except Pursah's usual "J" for "Jesus."

Logion 75 – Commentary on Content

Clearly, the special relationships[20] of the world are the substitute for our Holy Relationship with Jesus. (See also Logia 87 and 99, Commentaries on Content.) So as long as we hang on to those, we push Jesus out the door and prevent ourselves from being reunited with our true Self in the "marriage" of the spirit, the *only* marriage which can truly bring us joy.

---

20 Understanding the Course's concept of "special relationships" is crucial, because it is within the context of those persons/things we seek out in the ego-world, who/which serve in effect as scapegoats for our guilt, the purpose of which is to reaffirm our cherished separate individual (false) identities. Imagining that they solve our problems, they actually perpetuate conflict in the world, by our blaming everyone/everything for what befalls us. However, the Course's path is not one of rejecting our earthly relationships, but of learning to see them differently through forgiveness, so that the very relationships in which we engage become the very classroom where we learn to let go of the ego.

Logion 76

J said, "God's Divine Rule is like a merchant who had a supply of merchandise and then found a pearl. That merchant was prudent; he sold the merchandise and bought the single pearl for himself. So also with you, seek the treasure that is unfailing, that is enduring, where no moth comes to eat and no worm destroys."

Logion 76 - Comments on Form

- Here again, Pursah chooses "God's Divine Rule" over "the Father's Kingdom," and it is a phrase that, in some ways, seems more easily understandable.

Logion 76 – Commentary on Content

This mini-parable is yet another way of saying that the choice between the ego and the Holy Spirit is always one or the other. The thought system of the ego is one hundred percent hate and is ever-changing, and the thought system of the Holy Spirit is one hundred percent love and is eternal, and never the twain shall meet. Evidently, one is true and the other one is not, and it should become obvious which choice to make. The Course is there—Jesus is there—to help lead us out of the fog of unknowing in which we mistake hate ("special relationships") for love. When we wake up to the difference, the choice becomes easier. The only reason we stick to the ego, as we did and continue to do from the moment that we chose it, is because it is the "devil" we know, that is, we are comfortable with the familiar. It is stepping back from that decision with Jesus which lets the light shine in, and, as we will then see, it turns out that the emperor has no clothes on.

The same is expressed in many ways in the Course, and the process is designed to help us learn to make that choice as we become more discerning between the inner peace the Holy Spirit offers and the stress and anxiety of the ego's arsenal of worldly treasure.

Logion 79

A woman in the crowd said to him, "Lucky are the womb that bore you and the breasts that fed you." He said to her, "Lucky are those who have heard the word of the Father and have truly kept it. For there will be days when you will say, 'Lucky are the womb that has not conceived and the breasts that have not given milk.'"

Logion 79 - Comments on Form

- There is no structural change here, although it is always worthwhile to note Pursah's word choices, which are clearly very deliberate and precise.

Logion 79 – Commentary on Content

This saying exposes a typical ego fallacy, namely, that the past explains the present and makes us what we are, the foundation for such notions as "ancestor worship" and the Church's doctrine of the "apostolic succession." (See Logion 52, Commentary on Content.) The "blessing" it suggests here is to honor the past and ignore the present, which is precisely the ego's purpose. Jesus's answer is quite plainly that the "achievements" of the ego and/or our worldly antecedents have nothing whatsoever to contribute to who or what we are, ever. And so, while in the world the notion of having nursed a child—or any other accomplishment—might be a badge of merit for future reward, to Jesus the only thing that matters is the choice we make right now, since all there is is *this* "holy instant," in the eternal now. It has the same ring as his notion that those who do the Will of the Father are his family: he is about spiritual relations, not about earthly relations.

Logion 80

J said, "Whoever has come to know the world has discovered the body, and whoever has discovered the body, of that one the world is not worthy."

Logion 80 - Comments on Form

- Pursah again chooses her usual "J" for "Jesus."

Logion 80 – Commentary on Content

This statement equates the world with the body in a way familiar to Course students. The final comment suggests that, once you have seen through the world and the body, you are ready to leave the world. It has become meaningless, and it can no longer hold your attention. And because it is no longer worth anything to you, the world is not worthy of you. For the notion of the world not being worthy of us, refer to Logia 56, 85, and 111.

Logion 85

J said, "Adam came from great power and great wealth, but he was not worthy of you. For had he been worthy, he would not have tasted death."

Logion 85 - Comments on Form

- As always, Pursah prefers "J" for "Jesus."

Logion 85 – Commentary on Content

This statement adds up to another way of suggesting that, all in all, the separation was (is!) not such a wonderful idea, in line with the Course's reference to it as a "tiny, mad idea," and we could do better than choosing the ego thought system of death. Clearly, all of the seeming power that goes into the separation, here assigned to Adam as the primordial/archetypical first man, amounts to nothing. Looking at it this way, we are reminded that we are not the ego. (Cf. Logia 56, 80, and 111, commentaries on content.)

Logion 86

J said, "Foxes have their dens and birds have their nests, but human beings have no place to lay down and rest."

Logion 86 - Comments on Form

- Pursah chooses the usual "J" for "Jesus."

- She chooses a more contemporary expression, "human beings," in lieu of the archaic "the child of mankind," or variations thereof in the translations.

Logion 86 – Commentary on Content

The Course says: "Salvation is no more than a reminder this world is not your home." (ACIM:T-25.VI.6:1)

This saying could also remind us of the image: "You are at home in God, dreaming of exile but perfectly capable of awakening to reality." (ACIM: T-10.I.2:1) This latter text continues the image of a child sleeping safely in its crib at home, just having a bad nightmare of a distant land in which there is no such place to sleep safely.

Logion 87

J said, "How miserable is the body that depends on a body, and how miserable is the soul that depends on these two."

Logion 87 - Comments on Form

- Pursah exercises her normal preference of "J" for "Jesus," and there are no other changes.

Logion 87 – Commentary on Content

This statement would seem to be an early form of Jesus's teaching on special relationships versus the Holy Relationship and on communication. Namely, bodies cannot communicate. As anyone knows, physical closeness provides no assurance of wellbeing, despite all the elaborate illusions that the ego entertains to the contrary in this area, with its promises of happiness and fulfillment. Disillusionment and depression is the inevitable result. Real joining is only in joining with Jesus, through seeing the face of Christ in our brothers, and that has naught to do with depending on the body. Seen in that light, the attraction between bodies is purely an ego-distraction.

A useful Course reference is:

Only minds communicate. Since the ego cannot obliterate the impulse to communicate because it is also the impulse to create, it can only teach you that the body can both communicate and create, and therefore does not need the mind. (ACIM:T-7.V.2:1-2)

Logion 88

J said, "The messengers and the prophets will come to you and give you what belongs to you. You, in turn, give them what you have, and say to yourselves, 'When will they come and take what belongs to them?'"

Logion 88 - Comments on Form

- Pursah's usual preference of "J" for "Jesus."

Logion 88 – Commentary on Content

This saying offers an interesting parallel with the Course's teaching on the difference between the messengers of the world and Heaven's messengers:

> There is one major difference in the role of Heaven's messengers, which sets them off from those the world appoints. The messages that they deliver are intended first for them. And it is only as they can accept them for themselves that they become able to bring them further, and to give them everywhere that they were meant to be. Like earthly messengers, they did not write the messages they bear, but they become their first receivers in the truest sense, receiving to prepare themselves to give.
>
> An earthly messenger fulfills his role by giving all his messages away. The messengers of God perform their part by their acceptance of His messages as for themselves, and show they understand the messages by giving them away. They choose no roles that are not given them by His authority. And so they gain by every message that they give away.
>
> (ACIM:W-154.6-7)

Implicitly, it is also the answer to the "false prophets," who spend their time "hearing the Holy Spirit" (or whatever they call it), lording it over others, and telling everybody else what to do; of such, the comment has been made "do as I say, not as I do." Truth comes with humility, as the above passage from the Course suggests.

Logion 89

J said, "Why do you wash the outside of the cup? Don't you understand that the one who made the inside is also the one who made the outside?"

Logion 89 - Comments on Form

- Pursah again prefers "J" for "Jesus."

Logion 89 – Commentary on Content

Here is an early version of Jesus's teaching in the Course on the difference between content and form (see, for example, his wonderful analogy of the picture and the frame, ACIM:T-25.II.4-8), emphasizing that we are always preoccupied with things looking good (outside, the frame) and neglect or ignore the content (inside, the picture). Spirit, of course, "minds" only the content, not the form, which becomes purely incidental.

Logion 90

J said, "Come to me, for my yoke is comfortable and my lordship is gentle, and you will find rest for yourselves."

Logion 90 - Comments on Form

- "J" for Jesus.

- "Comfortable" as an adjective describing his "yoke," rather than "easy," or "gentle," as we find in some translations.

- "Lordship" in lieu of "mastery," which seems to reinforce respect for Jesus, which, according to the Course, an elder brother is entitled to (cf. ACIM:T-1.II.3:7). Some of the translators (e.g., Hebblethwaite, Pierre, Bethge, Weber) choose the term "lordship" as well, but most use words like "mastery" or "command."

Logion 90 – Commentary on Content

A variety of Course teachings come to mind, such as "Atonement without sacrifice" (ACIM:T-3.I), for the ego sees Jesus's total authority as a threat and projects that he will be a harsh taskmaster and we should stay out of his way. Jesus emphasizes, however, that his "yoke is comfortable." The point here is that his authority is based on love, unlike the ego's notion of authority, which is always based on usurping a false authority and therefore needs to be heavily defended.

The spirit in which this is said is the same as the Course's notion that "This is a course in mind training." (ACIM:T-1.VII.4:1), namely, the point of his teaching is that only with this kind of gentle discipline can we free our minds from the chaos of the ego thought system and return it to the peaceful thought system of the Holy Spirit. As the Course makes clear throughout, its goal is that we should become more peaceful, so this investment in gentle discipline (starting with remembering to ask for help from the Holy Spirit whenever we slip on another of the ego's banana peels) is the discipline of Jesus's non-judgment, versus the slavery to the ego's harsh judgments of sin, guilt, and fear.

Logion 91

They said to him, "Tell us who you are so that we may believe in you." He said to them, "You examine the face of Heaven and earth, but you have not come to know the one who is in your presence, and you do not know how to examine the present moment."

Logion 91 - Comments on Form

- Pursah chooses to capitalize "Heaven," in line with the usage found in *A Course in Miracles*.

Logion 91 – Commentary on Content

This little exchange exposes how, because it is rooted in the past, the ego cannot recognize the reality of spirit in the present. So, again, ego and spirit are two mutually exclusive thought systems. The ego has nothing to contribute to helping us recognize Jesus's presence in us, or else salvation would be under the ego's "imprimatur" and the ego would stay in charge, when the point is that we cease to take it seriously.

Logion 92

J said, "Seek and you will find. In the past, however, I did not tell you the things about which you asked me then. Now I am willing to tell them, but you are not seeking them."

Logion 92 - Comments on Form

- Pursah prefers "J" for "Jesus."

- No other major differences, except for variations in word choices among translations.

Logion 92 – Commentary on Content

This saying almost has the qualities of a Zen-koan. It is a cryptic way of pointing out some teachings that are familiar from the Course, contrasting the ego's seeking (outside), which guarantees that we will not find (ACIM:T-12.V.7:1), with the seeking that Jesus tells us to do (inside), which assures us that we will find. And once we have brought our question to the answer (ACIM:T-27.IV.7.5), there is nothing else to seek. It also expresses, in an interesting way, the notion that *we are really afraid to hear what Jesus has to say*, which closely relates to his insistence in the Course that he will only come at our invitation. Another way of expressing this is by saying that true prayer is always answered, but, as long as we entertain conflict, we continue to block the love, which alone can meet our needs.

Logion 94

J said, "One who seeks will find. And for one who knocks, it shall be opened."

Logion 94 - Comments on Form

• Pursah's version is very close to the translations here.

Logion 94 – Commentary on Content

On p. 80 of *The Disappearance of the Universe,* Pursah notes that this statement, along with Logion 95, are two more examples of NT "prequels." (See Index 2.) And she adds that she and Arten may occasionally refer to other NT sayings they feel were authentic, emphasizing that: "...but the meaning will not always be the same for us as you are generally used to thinking of it." The latter, of course, chimes in with the frequent corrections to the Bible and Christianity which Jesus offers in *A Course in Miracles,* especially in the early chapters. In other words, it is the Bible and Christianity which represent the deviation from his teachings. Typically, the way we misconstrue Jesus when we listen to him with our ego is always through level confusion, so that when he speaks of "bread," we visualize physical bread, never mind how often he reminds us that he was not speaking of those kinds of "breads," but rather was speaking in parables.

For the rest, this statement seems to convey reassurance, along the lines of the Course dictum, that "...the outcome is as certain as God." (ACIM:T-2.III.3:10) We may also be reminded of:

"Many are called but few are chosen" should be, "All are called but few choose to listen." Therefore, they do not choose right. The "chosen ones" are merely those who choose right sooner. Right minds can do this now, and they will find rest unto their souls. God knows you only in peace, and this *is* your reality. (ACIM:T-3.IV.7:12-16)

Logion 95

J said, "If you have money, do not lend it at interest. Rather, give it to someone who will not pay you back."

Logion 95 - Comments on Form

- Pursah has her usual "J" for "Jesus."

Logion 95 – Commentary on Content

Another NT "prequel." (See Index 2.) See the Commentary on Content to Logion 94 for Pursah's remarks.

This is an evident parallel to the Course's teaching that the ego's form of giving is "giving to get," in contrast with the spirit's laws of giving, in which we gain by giving, because we ourselves have to receive in order to give.

The following passage sums it up:

> Only those who have a real and lasting sense of abundance can be truly charitable. This is obvious when you consider what is involved. To the ego, to give anything implies that you will have to do without it. When you associate giving with sacrifice, you give only because you believe that you are somehow getting something better, and can therefore do without the thing you give. "Giving to get" is an inescapable law of the ego, which always evaluates itself in relation to other egos. (ACIM:T-4.II.6:1-5)

The statement is also a reminder that the results in the world, on the level of form, are not the object of the exercise. This is one of the great traps when we start on the path of forgiveness, that if we do not see the results, we attack ourselves, thinking we did not forgive perfectly, or we attack Jesus on the grounds of truth in advertising, saying that his Course does not work. As soon as we do this, we lose sight of the fact that it is the change of mind which matters. How and when it all works out in form is under the auspices of the Holy Spirit.

Logion 96

J said, "God's Divine Rule is like a woman. She took a little leaven, hid it in dough, and made it into large loaves of bread. Anyone here with two ears had better listen!"

Logion 96 - Comments on Form

• Here Pursah favors "God's Divine Rule" again.

• She makes a slight modification of the "ears to hear" quote, and

• She has the usual "J" for "Jesus."

Logion 96 – Commentary on Content

This statement is a very clear expression of the abundance of Heaven, of the Laws of God, and it foreshadows such stories as the "miracles" of the loaves and the fishes, which obviously are parables to express the same idea, namely, that spiritual nourishment always increases by our very acceptance of it and therefore is decidedly different from the so-called nourishment of the world, of which inevitably less is left (and someone else is deprived) when we partake of it. In other words, the ego's world of scarcity is a win/lose proposition; the spirit's world of abundance is a true win/win proposition.

Logion 97

J said, "God's Divine Rule is like a woman who was carrying a jar full of meal. While she was walking along a distant road, the handle of the jar broke, and the meal spilled behind her along the road. She didn't know it; she hadn't noticed a problem. When she reached her house, she put the jar down and discovered it was empty."

Logion 97 - Comments on Form

- Once more Pursah favors "God's Divine Rule."

- Otherwise only trivial changes.

Logion 97 – Commentary on Content

This statement is a play on the issues of content and form, and, in another way, it is an interesting corollary to the NT word "Seek first the Kingdom." If we focus on form, we will lose the content, and we will not even know it, but our whole trip will be in vain. Those are the typical disappointments that come from investing in the ways of the ego. Once we put the outside first, we will lose the inside. The fact that the handle of the jar broke off is also an important part of the image, for it is a metaphor that everything in the world of time and space is impermanent and destined to break down and decay. The ego's achievements are always pyrrhic victories.

Other statements in the Thomas gospel play on this same theme in different forms.

Logion 99

The disciples said to him, "Your brothers and your mother are standing outside." He said to them, "Those here who do what my Father wants are my brothers and my mother. They are the ones who will enter the Father's Kingdom."

Logion 99 - Comments on Form

- Pursah chooses "disciples"; some of the translations have "followers."

- She chooses capitalization of "Father" and "Kingdom."

- Curiously, while always consistent in content, Pursah is not consistent in her support for an improved version of the innovation from the Jesus Seminar, "God's Divine Rule," and sometimes reinforces the traditional language of "the Kingdom, "which, again, is also used throughout the Course.

Logion 99 – Commentary on Content

This saying is another one of Jesus's clear instructions on "special relationships" long before he coined the phrase for the Course. Very evidently, this statement highlights how our special relationships in the world serve merely as substitutes for our only real relationship, within the Holy Relationship, through the joining with Jesus in doing God's Will, which is the path of salvation— acceptance of the Atonement, in the Course's language. In addition to those specifically identified by Pursah in DU (pp. 79-80), this statement, too, is yet another "prequel" (see Index 2) to a word that is familiar from the NT.

Logion 100

They showed J a gold coin and said to him, "The Roman Emperor's people demand taxes from us." He said to them, "Give the Emperor what belongs to the Emperor. Give God what belongs to God."

Logion 100 - Comments on Form

- Besides a little modernization, the "Roman Emperor" is probably easier on the ear and reader comprehension than the traditional "Caesar."

- It is noteworthy that Pursah lops off the final words, which we find in the translations (typically: "and give me what is mine"), which intuitively sound odd right away and seem out of place.

Logion 100 – Commentary on Content

In the parlance of its day, this saying is the recipe for warning us against what was later to be called "level confusion" in the Course (e.g., Chapter 2 of the Text, passim). And it highlights the ego's strong tendency to always want to apply things on the physical plane, which is the reason why Jesus's teachings were constantly misunderstood. So, in the world, you do what everybody does, but you do not confuse the world with the realm of the spirit, which is what the ego always does by ascribing to form the power that only spirit has.

Logion 103

J said, "Congratulations to those who know where the rebels are going to attack. They can get going, collect their Divine resources, and be prepared before the rebels arrive."

Logion 103 - Comments on Form

- As always, Pursah writes "J" for "Jesus."

- For the rest, Pursah's edits give the statement a slightly more abstract tone, making it more easily generalizable.

Logion 103 – Commentary on Content

In a simple form, what this says is that, once you understand where the ego is coming from, you are always prepared for the way it attacks and you know where to go (right mind) for help in dealing with any situation that arises. The "rebels," obviously, are the ego's ragtag army of rebel rousers, disturbing the peace of Heaven, because they buy into the "tiny, mad idea," the Course's humorous term for the ego's central tenet of the separation.

We might note here that "generalization" is another concept the Course emphasizes throughout as a crucially important teaching/learning principle, whereby the student learns the basic principle of an idea, and, in the context of the specifics of his own life, he can then apply that principle to any particular situation that arises. (See, for example, ACIM:T-12.V.6:4 and W-In.4:2.)

Again, this is what Jesus clearly meant with his "follow me," to follow him in content, and we will understand his directive more and more as we learn to choose the miracle. The inner learning is in the growing recognition that the meaning of the stages of the path is indeed the same as that which he has shown us, except the specific circumstances are totally different. So different, in fact, that at first we have no clue to understanding anything; it is as though it only becomes clear to us in retrospect, for we had to be completely blind to our own circumstance before we can learn to make the choice between the ego and the Holy Spirit. This is also what he means to convey with the image in the Course that he is an elder brother who can show us the way.

Logion 106

J said, "When you make the two into one, you will become children of Adam, and when you say, 'Mountain, move from here!' it will move."

Logion 106 - Comments on Form

- Pursah makes minor changes, including the usual "J" for "Jesus," and some typography.

- Pursah uses a classical expression for the Sonship in the separation: "children of Adam" in lieu of "children of humanity" or "sons of man," as various translators have it.

Logion 106 – Commentary on Content

When we let go of the thought of being separate from God and the resulting conflict in our lives, the biggest obstacles in the world will dissolve in the face of the miracle. It is curious that Pursah should choose the expression "children of Adam," as the Course pointedly refers to the fact that nowhere in the Bible is there talk of Adam waking up after he falls asleep. (ACIM:T-2.I.3:6) But, of course, waking up from the dream of separation is exactly what *A Course in Miracles* is designed to help us do. As children of Adam, we all believed in the separation, but we now know there is "another way"(see Logion 48) of perceiving, which is in our power to choose. (ACIM:T-4.II.4.10) Perhaps her use of the name Adam here, who is, of course, the biblical first man, suggests this is another symbol for coming back to the beginning point, the Alpha, the decision point.

In Christianity, it is physical miracles which are deemed to inspire faith. In Jesus's teachings, it is our choice to accept the Atonement, which inspires the miracle, the shift of the mind from hell to Heaven. In other words, we need to change our mind first, whereas the emerging Christian model fully protects our inability to change our minds and makes us believe we are but miserable sinners, who have to wait for some external savior to come and get us when it pleases him.

Logion 107

J said, "God's Divine Rule is like a shepherd who had a hundred sheep. One of them, the largest, went astray. He left the ninety-nine and looked for the one until he found it. After he had toiled, he said to the sheep, 'I love you more than the ninety-nine.'"

Logion 107 - Comments on Form

- Evidently, Pursah feels that there were some embellishments here, and she strips the story down to the very basics.

Logion 107 – Commentary on Content

"All my brothers are special." (ACIM:T-1.V.3:6) This is Jesus's way of reassuring us, in a similar way in the Course, to counter the ego's panic that it will be annihilated and that this would be the end of us—which seems to be true, as long as we identify with the ego and believe that we are it.

Logion 108

J said, "Whoever drinks from my mouth shall become like me. I myself shall become that person, and the hidden things will be revealed to that person."

Logion 108 - Comments on Form

- Pursah makes no major changes, except the usual "J" for "Jesus," and her punctuation is different from that used in the translations.

Logion 108 – Commentary on Content

In one form at least, this is the clarification to the use of the word "hidden," which precedes the word "sayings," in the opening line of the Thomas gospel (Logion 1), making it clear that, indeed, it is not Jesus's intent to hide things from us and to hold out on us. Rather, we need to meet him on his terms and accept the truth from him on his terms before those hidden things can be revealed to us, because it is the ego's blindness which hides the vision of the Holy Spirit from us. If we hang on to our old frame of reference, then these "hidden" things cannot be revealed to us, because we hide them from ourselves. Eventually, we will appreciate that that is the very purpose of the ego thought system: to obliterate Jesus and keep our true identity from our awareness.

Logion 109

J said, "God's Divine Rule is like a person who had a treasure hidden in his field but did not know it. And when he died he left it to his son. The son did not know about it either. He took over the field and sold it. The buyer went plowing, discovered the treasure, and began to lend money at interest to whomever he wished."

Logion 109 - Comments on Form

• Pursah makes no substantive changes here.

Logion 109 – Commentary on Content

This saying is yet again another way of expressing the abundance of God's Kingdom and the fact that it is right here, right now. Yet, we are so busy with the things of the world that we miss it. The abundance it offers us far outstrips the ego's miserable concept of needs. It also is an interesting way of expressing that the Kingdom is in front of our faces (as also in Logion 113) and available to anyone who wants to do the inner work needed for its realization. Hence, *A Course in Miracles* is "a course in mind training," as the teaching of Jesus in this modern form announces itself. (ACIM:T-1.VII.4:1)

Logion 110

J said, "Let one who has found the world, and has become wealthy, renounce the world."

Logion 110 - Comments on Form

- Pursah again has "J" for "Jesus" and makes the sentence run more smoothly.

Logion 110 – Commentary on Content

This saying is yet another expression of the idea that it is our attachments in the world which hold us back. We should also note that this is another saying that should not be taken literally, which is what the world always tries to do in order to kill Jesus's meaning. Every good lawyer knows that you can kill the intent of the law by taking it literally. In other words, this is not an encouragement to unleash Armageddon and destroy the world, as some apocalyptic faiths would have us believe. Nor is it about giving anything up in the world, but it is simply about giving up our *attachments* to the things of the world.

In growing up and becoming "responsible adults," we learn the ways of the world (the Course's "Laws of Chaos," as found in Chapter 23, Section II), only to discover we made a Faustian bargain, and we have become "wealthy" in terms of the "sharp-edged children's toys" (cf. ACIM:W-pII.4.5:2) of the separation, so that at this point we are spiritual children. By then choosing "another way" (see Logion 48), we can embark on a path of spiritual growth, in which we give up those toys, which only hurt us. In essence, everything of this world is such a sharp-edged toy for the simple fact of the win/lose nature of the world, so whatever I have, you do not, and this sets me apart from you, and vice versa. So these worldly belongings, both abstract and physical, are used as proof of differences and separation, and therein lies their sharp edge. Once we see this, we must realize that it is not like the old saw, that he who has the most toys wins, but rather the one who recognizes the worthlessness of all the toys of the world.

Logion 111

J said, "The Heavens and the earth will roll up in your presence, and whoever is living with the living one will not see death. Did not I say, 'Those who have found themselves, of them the world is not worthy'?"

Logion 111 - Comments on Form

- Pursah chooses the usual "J" for "Jesus."

- She restores here the original form as a saying, leaving off the third-party construct in the second part of the statement.

Logion 111 – Commentary on Content

Along with an allusion to an earlier statement, here is another way of expressing that we need to seek the answers inside, not outside. The way this Logion is phrased sounds interestingly like the title of a recent book, *The Disappearance of the Universe*. The point is that this world of appearances will cease to exist eventually as we awaken to our Immortal Reality, to stay with another term Gary Renard has chosen for a book title.

Here we find once again the notion that the world (made up by the ego, not created by God) is not worthy of us once we wake up to what we truly are. (Cf. Logia 56, 80 and 85, commentaries on content.)

Logion 113

The disciples said to him, "When will the Kingdom come?" He said, "It will not come by watching for it. It will not be said, 'Behold here,' or 'Behold there.' Rather, the Kingdom of the Father is spread out upon the earth, and people do not see it."

Logion 113 - Comments on Form

- Pursah prefers "disciples" in lieu of "followers," as some translations have it.

- She inserts "He said" before the obvious Jesus quote.

- She says "Behold" instead of "Look," as some translations say.

Logion 113 – Commentary on Content

In *The Disappearance of the Universe,* the comment on this saying is framed as follows (Pursah speaking):

> For as you can see from saying 113, J was teaching that the Kingdom of Heaven is something that is *present,* if not presently in your awareness. [saying 113 follows]
>
> J is not saying here that the Kingdom of the Father is *in* the earth. Indeed, he knew that the earth was in our minds. He was speaking about something that people do not see because the Kingdom of Heaven cannot *be* seen with the body's eyes, which are only capable of beholding limited symbols. Heaven does not exist within the realm of perception, but is the genuine form of life that you will eventually become completely *aware* of.
>
> (DU pp. 78-79)

Pursah continues to explain how we have lost our awareness of Heaven, and yet it is still within us, even if buried in the recesses of our mind. And she then clarifies that she and Arten are there to help Gary with his remembering process and that through him they can help others as well. From there, the discussion segues to sayings 26, 31, 36, 54, four of the Logia that Pursah specifically identifies as NT "prequels."

An Epilogue

Dear Reader,

I am leaving you with an unfinished work, unfinished in the spirit of the opening paragraph of this book, in that it is a beginning, not an end. Unfinished, because I cannot finish it for you. The real work for each of us is in developing our own relationship with Jesus, for which the 70, or 71 (depending on how you count the combination of Logia 6 and 14), sayings from Thomas can be a help, in the same vein as *A Course In Miracles* can be a help. The real work is in the *application* of what the Course teaches and in the following of Jesus in deed, not in word. These musings about the sayings of the Thomas gospel should spark— rather than limit—your own exploration of their meaning, which will grow with experience, quite as Pursah suggests, and their koan-like appearance should stimulate that inner process.

Pursah points out that this collection of sayings is not any kind of a spiritual masterwork per se, and it certainly lacks any coherent presentation of the teachings we are familiar with from the Course today. However, our exploration here can hopefully be helpful in appreciating the oneness of the thought system of what Jesus taught then and now, and always. Equally importantly, throughout the conversations in Gary Renard's two books, it is clear that Pursah and Arten also emphasize that the apostles did not necessarily understand Jesus at the time; from that point of view, the Thomas tradition of pure, unadulterated sayings was free of the distortions of subsequent interpretation. Relative to that, we should note that the books that later formed the NT Canon are editorialized and full of interpretation, culminating in efforts such as the books of Luke and Acts, which originally were one book and are both a product of Paul's secretary and conceived as a justification of the Pauline notions of Christianity.

Allowing yourself to become more and more comfortable with

the imagery of the sayings may open up another way of under-standing your own relationship with Jesus. We may not all have clear experiences along the lines Gary Renard alludes to having (in the form of recollections of a lifetime with Jesus) or like those of General Patton, who had clear recollections of roaming the battlefields of history in other incarnations. However, if you have read the book to this point, you are not interested in its material by accident, as there are no accidents in creation. So it is important to honor our deep attraction to these teachings and let them lead us to where they want to take us, not just in any direction of which we have pre-determined the relevance to us. Jesus is leading us out of this world we think we are caught up in, and it is time to follow our heart. He is showing us the way. It is up to us to follow him.

In this context, it would also pay to note again that, while we may not all have experiences similar to those of Gary Renard in the literal sense, his story is a practical demonstration of the holographic nature of this time-space experience, entirely in line with the teachings of the Course on this point, which calls all of time and space a "sleight of hand" (ACIM:W-158.4). Gary's confer-ences with his past and future self (Pursah), and the triangular relationships which span incarnations with his former friend (as Thaddeus, when Gary/Pursah was Thomas), future significant other (?—maybe in this life—who is Arten?[21]), and future husband (next life—Pursah), are a living reminder to us all to take our identities in this life much less seriously and be open to seeing our true Self reflected in all of our brothers.

I do believe that, in spending time with these unique sayings, we can get in touch at a deep level with feelings of familiarity which can make it at least more credible that perhaps "we were

---

21 This alludes to a metaphysical cliffhanger the book *Your Immortal Reality* left us with, namely, that Arten may be reappearing now, in Gary's present life, but this had not yet happened at the time of the publication of *Your Immoral Reality*. This mystery should be resolved in the sequel to that book, which is due to appear shortly after this one, in the fall of 2008.

there." The point is that, again, within the holographic model of our time-space experience which the Course espouses, it should be more natural to us to think that all of human experience—like Gary Renard's own experiences which he shares in his books—is really part of us, although within this particular lifetime, we may be more aware of certain roles than of others. And so Pursah may be offering us these sayings in this spirit of helping our recollection, as they bring up that faint ring of truth and familiarity with increasing clarity as we let them roll around in our minds and do their work to bring back memories.

The Course describes itself with terms like "simple" and "practical," and, again, the Workbook of the Course emphasizes the *application* of its principles throughout. Gary Renard's books, besides a lot of other things, show us a brother who is living the application of the Course for all to see through his books and workshops. And the one application is forgiveness, and more forgiveness, including of ourselves (always, really!), particularly whenever we think we did not do our lessons perfectly, for that also is a trap. While the Course appeals to the intellect, intellectual mastery may give us a helping hand in the understanding of the Course's metaphysics and so forth, but mastery at that level is merely the booby prize, for it then really becomes an ego design to prevent us from practicing what it says when we convince ourselves that we already understand it. At that point, what we are really doing is following the ego as our guide—the very thought choice that got us into this insane mess in the first place—instead of the Holy Spirit, without Whose help we cannot awaken from this "fool-proof, but...not God-proof" nightmare. (ACIM:T-5.VI.10:6)

Historically, Christianity set the precedent, from the moment Paul started his revisionist interpretation of Jesus, which ultimately became more important than the real thing. As the German saying goes: "Ganz wie echt, nur besser." (Just like the real thing, only better.) So much so, that a good part of Jesus's sayings in the Thomas collection were nearly completely obliterated from the historical record. The period of the first few decades of the Course's existence has been rife with a wide variety of would-be Course teachers who did little but compromise the materials and make themselves important, as if the Course were in need of interpretation. The Course is in need of application, not interpretation.

So then as now, if teachers become more important than the teaching, we go off on tangents. Ken Wapnick frequently likes to remind his audiences that there is nothing in the Course that speaks about study groups or workshops, because it is a self-study course. Yet, if such gatherings are helpful to you, by all means use them, without forgetting the real purpose is practicing the Course, beginning with forgiving the person next to you who may have a nervous habit or some other thing going on which irritates you, or the one in the back with the stupid questions, or the one who monopolizes the conversations or tries to make it a debating club about the merits of the Course instead of a workshop on the Course, and so on. The Course's unique contribution to spirituality is that it makes clear, as does the Thomas gospel, that it is whatever is in front of our face which always provides us our best classroom and our shortest journey home, if we can only learn to ask for help from the Holy Spirit instead of the ego.

The Course says:

Time is a trick, a sleight of hand, a vast illusion in which figures come and go as if by magic. Yet there is a plan behind appearances that does not change. The script is written. When experience will come to end your doubting has been set. For we but see the journey from the point at which it ended, looking back on it, imagining we make it once again; reviewing mentally what has gone by. (ACIM:W-158.4) and:

> The Holy Spirit, the shared Inspiration of all the Sonship, induces a kind of perception in which many elements are like those in the Kingdom of Heaven itself:
>
> First, its universality is perfectly clear, and no one who attains it could believe for one instant that sharing it involves anything but gain.
>
> Second, it is incapable of attack and is therefore truly open. This means that although it does not engender knowledge, it does not obstruct it in any way.
>
> Finally, it points the way beyond the healing that it brings, and leads the mind beyond its own integration toward the paths of creation. It is at this point that sufficient quantitative change occurs to produce a real qualitative shift.
>
> (ACIM:T-5.I.7)

We might conclude here with Logion 5, remembering with the Course that whatever our present circumstance, it is always the best "classroom":

> Know what is in front of your face, and what is hidden from you will be disclosed to you. For there is nothing hidden that will not be revealed.

Beyond that, I can only hope that this book will be helpful to the reader in "closing the circle" in their own experience and in seeing the connection between the original teachings of Jesus, as we find them in the Thomas gospel and its modern counterpart, *A Course in Miracles*. Gary Renard's work established that connection, and this book can hopefully contribute to a deepening understanding of it. On another level, "closing the circle" could just as easily refer to the experience that the thought system the Course teaches us is not alien to us at all. We know it, and we are just remembering it. It is inner recognition which connects our Course work with our experience and brings about the remembering of what the ego wants us to forget, which is that Jesus never left us. In those moments of recognition, which the Course calls the "miracle," he is present with us. To stick more closely to Course metaphysics, we never left our home in Heaven; we just had a nightmare and temporarily forgot who we are.

The latter is perhaps the key point. Christianity historically chose to side with the notion that the resurrection came after the crucifixion. It is because Christianity was so focused on Jesus's body, and his life in the world, that it became increasingly bothered by the appearance of his leaving and had the faithful waiting for his return in the Second Coming,[22] resulting in considerable difficulty when he did not stick to their schedule. Jesus's point was, rather, that he never left and would always be present for us whenever we invite him in.

With the Course, we would understand—as did some early Christian groups—that the moment of Jesus's baptismal experience (in terms of the Gospels), when he hears the Voice for God say: "Thou art my beloved Son, in whom I am well pleased," was in fact the moment of the resurrection and is thus the beginning of his ministry on earth, as the Gospel of Mark recognizes. Anything prior to that is irrelevant from that point of view, and obviously we can trace the beginning of mythmaking to Matthew and Luke when they add stories about his life before that time. That is the moment when we remember who we are as the one Son of God, as opposed to believing we are the false self, which is our made-up identity in this world. And so Jesus's baptism marks the moment his ministry began. The resurrection in that light is merely his appearance in a body after his death and

---

22 The student of early Christian history will find that there were numerous episodes of theological adjustments to accommodate the continuing delay of this version of the Second Coming. This is, in fact, still going on today, with an almost unending series of rationalizations, mostly connected to eschatological expectations, as with the current craze of "the rapture."

is a different experience for different people.

In this remembering of the thought system of the Holy Spirit, of the right mind, it is then that we truly begin to live with an awareness that Jesus is closer to us than anything and that it is really up to us to let him in. He never left. Better yet, we never left. All is forgiven. Nothing ever happened to disturb the peace of Heaven. God's Son is innocent and free.

Appendix 1

In *Your Immortal Reality*, there is a quote of a piece I once contributed to the on-line forum on *The Disappearance of the Universe* (DU-group) at Yahoo.com, and I gave Gary Renard permission to include it in that book. At the time, I repressed the urge to edit that text, for the sake of historical accuracy. In the context of this book, however, I think it merits reprinting the piece, but with some minor edits, as well as a concluding note, and some other materials. Clearly, writing on a forum on the Internet is not done with the same kind of reflection and care as writing a book.

The prototype of the following segment can be found on pages 157-159 of *Your Immortal Reality*. It was my response to a comment on that same list by a self-professed Christian who had difficulty with the concept of Jesus in *The Disappearance of the Universe*.

Hi. Just consider that different people have experienced J in different ways. Christianity explains J in a certain way, and if that works for you, you should stick with it. However, those explanations do not work for a lot of people, including my parents, who left their church when I was two and a half years old. One of the realizations they had, which surfaced repeatedly in Protestant theological discussions since the middle of the 19th century, was that Christianity was a creation of Paul and did not represent the teachings of J. Subsequently, I was raised with a notion of the living presence of J in my life, in the form of our ability to call on him as "God's Help." So for me, the idea of J dying for our sins was always phony baloney; it was a made-up

231

theology about J, as opposed to a teaching of J.

Then, when I found *A Course in Miracles,* where J explains in detail why the meaning of the crucifixion is NOT the sacrifice of God's son for our sins, but is rather a teaching of infinite love, I knew that this was the J for whom I had been looking all of my life. There was a profound recognition. All my life, I had studied scripture quite intensely, including studying the Old Testament in Hebrew and the New Testament in Greek, so as not to have to depend on translations I did not trust. Plus, I frankly always focused on the words of J, not on the interpretations of others, such as Paul and even the apostles. Even from the stories in the New Testament, it seemed clear to me that the apostles were struggling to understand him and were by no means clear about his meaning. The apparent certainty and seeming clarity of Paul for me always seemed to be a cover over a profound uncertainty concerning his own experience on the road to Damascus. So for me, Paul always seemed unreliable in the extreme. He writes beautiful passages, but they are framed within a lot of hateful stuff about sin and guilt, not to mention the biggest ones: his interpretation of the crucifixion as J dying for our sins and his emphasis on proselytizing, in lieu of teaching by example.

In short, for me J worked, Paul did not, and, in *A Course in Miracles* and later *The Disappearance of the Universe,* I found the voice of J free of the later theologies about him. Also, I was aware very early of the Gospel according to Thomas, from which J speaks to us in terms which are very clearly non-dualistic, and which produce great difficulty in harmonizing them with Pauline theology, though there is potentially less of a problem with other gospel materials, depending on how you read those. The churches initially tried to dismiss the Thomas gospel as being rather late, but internal evidence has led many scholars to date these sayings rather early, in fact, probably ca. 50 CE, or long *before* the letters of Paul or the other Gospels were even written. In which case it offers interesting additional evidence of the teachings of J free of the later Pauline theologizing and distortion.

So, speaking strictly for myself, this makes sense to me and can be understood completely within a fairly orderly revisionist history of early Christianity. In this context, it should be clear that J had no intention whatsoever of founding a religion, but that rather he was a universal spiritual teacher, though appearing in a Jewish world. Seen in that light, Christianity was merely one attempt (even if it was to become historically dominant for 2,000 years) at framing those teachings as an organized religion. Looking at it this way, there is room for a different understanding of J, as exemplified by some of the many forms of Christianity that were ultimately suppressed, destroyed, and forgotten. This is represented today by a living tradition of great clarity which can be found in *A Course in Miracles* and *The Disappearance of the Universe.* Throughout history, other traditions have emerged from the shadows of Christianity to reflect the light of Jesus's teachings as a tradition of inner wisdom and spiritual growth.

Generally, the best idea will be to stick with what works for you. The model of *A Course in Miracles* works for me, and it is the topic of *The Disappearance of the Universe.* It is what is being discussed on this list. So if you are interested, hang around, but if not, that is fine too. No one here is interested in repeating any of the 2,000 years of infighting and splits which is the history of the Christian Church. We simply focus on an alternative view of the matter, which, again, is represented by *A Course in Miracles. The Disappearance of the Universe* adds to this by providing the bridge between the modern formulations of the teachings of J as presented in *A Course in Miracles* and the central teachings of the Thomas gospel. This is intriguing, since Thomas clearly does not fit comfortably within the Pauline tradition and presents major challenges to its theology. So, at a minimum, one would have to conclude that his gospel represented a different understanding of J from the figure orthodox Christianity developed.

Appendix 2

As I have emphasized throughout this book, the upshot of our new understanding about the early history of Christianity is not about making anyone wrong. Clearly, some people have found their path to enlightenment within the framework of the Church as well as outside of it, which makes sense to us as Course students on the basis of the fact that we are remembering a truth that is within us already, not learning something new that comes from outside.

However, what is very helpful to understand on a deeper and deeper level is how almost all of the early forms of Christianity distorted the teachings of Jesus one way or another, and when we do start to understand these histories they can be a mirror for us in terms of how our ego struggles to stay ahead of Jesus and render him harmless, since the thought system he does represent threatens the ego. No one indeed can serve two masters. We need to be vigilant at all times for the ego's attempts to foster compromise and to somehow reassert itself.

Historically, it was very symbolic that Christianity experienced success as a religion through its adoption by the Emperor Constantine "the Great" in 313, and finally in 380 under the Emperor Theodosius I, becoming the official religion of the Roman Empire. Thus, in what has got to be the ultimate contradiction in terms, Christianity compromised the teachings of Jesus to make them serviceable to Caesar.[23] If nothing else, those events should teach us what Christianity is not, namely, the teachings of Jesus.

In theological circles, the controversy about Paul has flared up

---

23   Perhaps the most interesting account to date of this process of the slide of the teachings of the Prince of Peace to the point of becoming the official religion of the Roman Empire is in the book *The Fall of Christianity* by the Dutch theologian Prof. G. J. Heering (see Bibliography). (Note that the English edition has been out of print for a long time.) What Heering did not understand was that the corruption started right away with Paul. Furthermore, he died before the Thomas gospel began to be well understood.

again and again, particularly in the last two hundred years, and it is amazing the degree to which we almost universally find that Paul is always again being reaffirmed by the theologians in the end. Amazing that is, until you realize that Christianity is Paul's theology, not Jesus's teaching, and thus it only makes sense that Christianity should reaffirm Paul, since he founded it. Many others, however, again and again have been bothered by the apparent contradictions between Jesus and Paul, none perhaps as famous as Thomas Jefferson, though he kept these notions mostly to himself in his lifetime.

We may note that in the Jefferson Bible itself, and in some of his correspondence on the topic, Jefferson shows clearly that he saw Paul's letters as an obfuscation—not a clarification—of the teachings of Jesus, and even if his understanding of Jesus was not closely in line with the Course, nevertheless his intuition on this point was wonderful. We might also note that the Jefferson Bible retains parallel passages to substantial portions of the Thomas gospel (some estimate it as high as seventy-five percent), which makes sense, if we compare them to the proportions found in the canonical literature: forty-seven in Mark, seventeen in Luke, four in Matthew, forty in Q, and five in John (cf. *The Five Gospels*, p. 15). The reason Jefferson's high correlation to Thomas makes sense is because the "sayings" he clipped from the Bible were predominantly Thomas in thought. The implication is also that anyone throughout history had the same freedom Jefferson did, i.e., the freedom to ignore a lot of the packaging of Jesus's teachings by subsequent tradition. In the simplest terms, it comes down to this: was Jesus what he taught, or was he the stories that were woven around him—however well intended—from 20 to 100 or more years after his death?

The following letter from Jefferson contains some choice words where he dispenses with Paul, and his unvarnished language probably explains the deliberate exclusion of parts of this material from the Jefferson Bible in the edition I used:

Letter To William Short

Monticello, April 13, 1820

DEAR SIR,

Your favor of March the 27th is received, and as you request, a copy of the syllabus is now enclosed. It was originally written to Dr. Rush. On his death, fearing that the inquisition of the public might get hold of it, I asked the return of it from the family, which they kindly complied with. At the request of another friend, I had given him a copy. He lent it to his friend to read, who copied it, and in a few months it appeared in the Theological Magazine of London. Happily that repository is scarcely known in this country, and the syllabus, therefore, is still a secret, and in your hands I am sure it will continue so.

But while this syllabus is meant to place the character of Jesus in its true and high light, as no impostor Himself, but a great Reformer of the Hebrew code of religion, it is not to be understood that I am with Him in all His doctrines. I am a Materialist; he takes the side of Spiritualism; he preaches the efficacy of repentance towards forgiveness of sin; I require counterpoise of good works to redeem it, etc., etc. It is the innocence of His character, the purity and sublimity of His moral precepts, the eloquence of His inculcations, the beauty of the apologues in which He conveys them, that I so much admire; sometimes, indeed, needing indulgence to eastern hyperbolism. My eulogies, too, may be founded on a postulate which all may not be ready to grant. Among the sayings and discourses imputed to Him by His biographers, I find many passages of fine imagination, correct morality, and of the most lovely benevolence; and others, again, of so much ignorance, so much absurdity, so much untruth, charlatanism and imposture, as to pronounce it impossible that such contradictions should have proceeded from the same Being. I separate, therefore, the gold from the dross; restore to Him the former, and leave the latter to the stupidity of some, and roguery of others of His disciples. Of this band of dupes and impostors, Paul was the great Coryphaeus and first corrupter of the doctrines of Jesus. These palpable interpolations and falsifications of His doctrines, led me to try to sift them apart. I found the work obvious and easy, and that His past composed the most beautiful morsel of morality which has been given to us by man. The syllabus is therefore of His doctrines, not all of mine. I read them as I do those of other ancient and modern moralists, with a mixture of approbation and dissent...

The edition of the Jefferson Bible that I hold in my hands dates from 1989 and has an introduction by the Rev. Forrest Church, pastor of All Souls Unitarian Church in New York City and son of former Senator Frank Church of Idaho; it also has an afterword by Jaroslav Pelikan, the famous historian of Christianity. Interestingly, Church's introduction does have most of the above letter, except that it is truncated after "and roguery of others of his disciples," leaving the very relevant justification for the elimination of Paul's writings from the Jefferson Bible out altogether, without even mentioning it or indicating with an ellipsis that the letter is abridged. It may seem like a small detail, but it is indicative of the routine burial of any doubts about Paul's interpretative influences in the Christian tradition, reaffirming always that Christianity, while claiming that its doctrines reflect the teaching of Jesus, was in fact shaped by the teaching of Paul more so than that of Jesus.

Besides that blatant omission, the afterword by Jaroslav Pelikan makes it even more interesting. He does account for the fact that Jefferson, like many other figures of the Enlightenment, thought that the teachings of Jesus had been compromised beyond recognition by Paul in the formation of Christianity.

However, why should Pelikan be so taken aback by what he describes in the afterword as *the sangfroid exhibited by the third president of the United States as, razor in hand, he sat editing the Gospels during February 1804, on (as he himself says) "2. or 3. nights only at Washington, after getting thro' the evening task of reading the letters and papers of the day."* He was apparently quite sure that he could tell what was genuine and what was not in the transmitted text of the New Testament, and the eventual outcome of his research and reflection is presented here in this volume. In this afterword, Pelikan goes on to discuss the basis of Jefferson's feelings about Paul as a corrupter of Jesus's teachings, quoting the very words from the letter cited above which Church has omitted without properly indicating it, let alone explaining it, in his introduction to the book.

Why, indeed, would anyone take offense, unless their default assumption is that Christianity is the real thing and Paul and his theology are to be accepted without question? After all, what Jefferson did was nothing more than to: (1) read the historical accounts; (2) guided by common sense and intuition, deduce what the actual statements of the teacher were; and (3) extricate them from the surrounding editorial material and narrative, all in order to get an unencumbered picture of the actual original teaching. Granted, he did dismiss a few Jesus quotes also, because he suspected corruption, and we might disagree with some of his choices today, but overwhelmingly his results hold up.

Given the high degree of correlation of Jefferson's editorial achievements with the Thomas gospel as noted earlier, he apparently did a creditable job, which demonstrates that anyone at any time could in the same way have mentally "filtered" Jesus out from the traditional sources. (No doubt there were, throughout history, those who managed to do just that very thing in their own self study and seeking, but we just will not hear from them without a written record.) This notion becomes all the more reasonable if we understand that the real process is a remembering of a truth that is within us at all times. So while at one time that remembering might take the form of sifting out Jesus's teachings from the traditions about him, today the form might be that we find ourselves drawn to *A Course in Miracles* and becoming a follower of Jesus through studying its curriculum. But we do not learn who Jesus is or what he teaches from those sources. That is an inner process, which simply takes form in our lives in such ways as are appropriate to the times in which we live and the specifics of our various life circumstances.

What makes the Jefferson Bible so interesting is that Thomas Jefferson performed his editing task while explicitly declaring that he did not necessarily agree with Jesus, by not sharing his spiritual viewpoint as he perceived it, since he felt himself to be a materialist. Nevertheless, he acknowledged the greatness of the teaching and sorted the wheat from the chaff with remarkable perceptiveness and mental acuity. The corollary to the book that resulted is a more stark understanding of the nature of Paul's influence and distortions, just by a process of elimination.

Over the years, I have found many expressions of the problems surrounding Paul and his role in founding Christianity, starting from the suspicious-sounding and sudden Saul/Paul conversion. The world tends to consider the flip-flop conversion from Saul to Paul on the road to Damascus, after he had his visionary experience of Jesus, as a signature conversion experience and a validation of his seriousness and genuineness. The experience may have been ever so valid and startling, but what he subsequently did with it may be open to some doubt. Psychologically, it should be readily obvious that this sort of bi-polar switching to the other side of the same issue is not a resolution, but stays within the problem dynamic as two sides of the same coin. It therefore does not undo the problem, but reaffirms it. Spiritual maturity would transcend the issue by understanding that both affirmation and rejection would continue to make the problem real, while truth always transcends it. Furthermore, proselytizing is always founded in insecurity, as it seeks a substitute for certainty in the power of numbers.

At various times in recent years, I found myself discussing these types of experiences with some friends, and, at some point, referred to them as "premature enlightenment," recognizing that they are a very common syndrome in which the spiritual seeker seeks to capitalize on a partial vision of the truth and then passes it off as the whole truth. This is usually accomplished by proselytizing behavior founded on manifestly false claims of universality—manifestly false since, if such claims were universal, no one would have to be convinced in the first place. Only truth is true and everything else, of necessity, is a lie, and so anyone who knows truth would not worry about anyone else doing so either, since the limited validity of lies eventually must exhaust itself, though no one gives up a favored lie until they tire of it themselves—try convincing your kids prematurely that there is no Santa Claus. *A Course in Miracles* is extraordinarily helpful in making us see that our forgetting or denying of the truth has had no effect whatsoever on Reality, and the Course expresses this idea on many levels. For example, in "...not one note in Heaven's song was missed." (ACIM:T-26.V.5:4), which simply denies everything the Son thinks he has done and feels guilty about. It is purely and only the cleaning up of this guilt, the cleaning of the Augias stables that the Course has us do, that will eventually make space for a truth that already is, regardless of our digressions.

To date, I have found no clearer discussion of this syndrome anywhere in the literature than in Nouk Sanchez and Tomas Vieira's book, *Take Me To Truth* (see Bibliography), where on page 162 the authors provide a diagram of the Course's stages of the "Development of Trust" (ACIM:M-4.I.A), which depicts a "bypass" to stage four from stage two, which is exactly the problem: we run with a momentary flash of insight, seeking to escape from the next stage of the process, stage three, which is the relinquishment of the ego's coveted sacred cows. They go on to discuss this issue extensively in the text of the book as well. It boils down to skipping over steps in the process and avoiding the questioning of all the unexamined values which uphold the ego system. The experience is one in which our ego, always happy to co-opt our spiritual path, gets back in charge (since it is staring bankruptcy in the face) and seizes on a glimpse of truth. It then substitutes a partial truth it can endorse and control for the real thing. In a workshop in New York City on October 6, 2007, Tomas used the term "trading on" such an insight, which struck me as a very powerful description of this phenomenon, for it is at this junction that cults, religions, and spiritual schools are founded. Here the ego and the world reaffirm themselves and derail spiritual progress by building a mausoleum and thus preventing further progress. This is where, in lieu of enlightenment, we open up a souvenir stand at some halfway point and make a living out of selling trinkets, instead of continuing on our journey. In the context of the canonical Gospels, this process is also indicated by scenes in which the crowds around Jesus make it hard to get to him, such as the scene in Mark 2:1-4, where a paralytic needs to be lifted through the roof to be brought to Jesus and be healed, because people were blocking the way to the house.

Simply put: there is no substitute for our own process, which is different in detail for everyone, since we all come into this life with different predispositions and karmic burdens. So while conceptually the path is the same for everyone, the details are always unique and different. In the Course's terms, to "question every value that you hold" (ACIM:T-24.in.2:1) is always different in form for different people since clearly we all have different values we hold on to. We all resist ferociously and prematurely claim victory. Substituting a picture postcard for the truth is a perfect ego strategy to get us to stop the process of ego demolition, as Nouk and Tomas refer to it. With a little luck, we may even have the option of becoming important as teachers and, in the process, make a career out of holding up the progress of others with our visions. As a spiritual path, the Course offers clear guidance to lead us out of this trap by insisting that it is a self-study program: "It is not intended to become the basis for another cult. [Thus Jesus is the only teacher in the eyes of the Course, and the facilitator of a workshop should not seek to usurp that authority.] Its only purpose is to provide a way in which some people will be able to find their own Internal Teacher." (From the "How It Came" section in the Preface to the Course; bracketed material is my addition.) Thus, it puts the onus back on us to do our own homework, since merely mouthing second-hand truths handed down from others is an obvious defense against the truth. As the Buddhist saying goes: "What is known as the teachings of the Buddha, are not the teachings of the Buddha."

Seen in this light, then, the phenomenon of Paul and the founding of Christianity is only an obvious ego response, since it perfectly serves the ego's purpose of hijacking a teaching that says that the world and the body are not real. All of us embarking on a serious spiritual path will find ourselves many times falling for this temptation, and until we understand the fear that drives us to do this, we will not let go of our cherished images, which Jesus in the Course refers to as "bitter idols" (ACIM:C-5.5:7). Once we realize that they merely delay us on our way and prolong the pain, we may be motivated to let them go.

Bibliography and Further Reading

A Course in Miracles, Foundation for Inner Peace, 1975-1996. Note: in 2007 the Foundation published the third edition, which includes two supplements to the Course: *Psychotherapy: Purpose, Process and Practice*, and *The Song of Prayer*. Both were originally published separately; having them presently in one volume makes this the preferred edition of the Course.

Gary R. Renard, *The Disappearance of the Universe: Straight Talk about Illusions, Past Lives, Religion, Sex, Politics, and the Miracles of Forgiveness*, Hay House, 2003.

Gary R. Renard, *Your Immortal Reality: How to Break the Cycle of Birth and Death*, Hay House, 2006.

Marvin Meyer, *The Gospel of Thomas: The Hidden Sayings of Jesus*, HarperSanFrancisco, 1992.

Robert W. Funk, Roy W. Hoover, and the Jesus Seminar, *The Five Gospels: What Did Jesus Really Say?*, Harper Collins, 1993.

R.T. France, *The Gospel of Mark* volume in *The New International Greek Testament Commentary* series, Eerdmans, 2002.

Jan Willem Kaiser, *Beleving van het Evangelie*, H.J.W. Becht, Amsterdam, 1950.

Robert K. Brown and Philip W. Comfort (Trs.) and J.D. Douglas (Ed.), *The New Greek-English Interlinear New Testament*, Tyndale House, 1990.

Elaine Pagels, *Beyond Belief: The Secret Gospel of Thomas*, Random House, 2003.

Jean-Yves Leloup, *The Gospel of Thomas: The Gnostic Wisdom of Jesus*, Inner Traditions, 2005, originally *L'Évangile de Thomas*, Albin Michel, 1986.

Benjamin Hebblethwaite and Jacques Pierre (Eds.), Hans-Gebbard Bethge and Michael Weber (Trs.), *The Gospel of Thomas, in English, Haitian Creole and French*, Classic Editions, Gainesville, Florida, 2005.

Hyam Maccoby, *The Mythmaker: Paul and the Invention of Christianity*, HarperSanFrancisco, 1986; reprint Barnes & Noble Books, 1998.

Arthur Drews, *The Christ Myth* (tr. from German by C. Deslisle Burns), Prometheus Press, 1998 (reprint of 1910 edition at Open Court, Chicago).

Thomas Jefferson, *The Jefferson Bible*, Forrest Church, Ed., Beacon Press, 1989.

Kenneth Wapnick, Ph.D., *A Talk Given On A Course in Miracles: An Introduction*, Foundation for *A Course in Miracles*, 1983-1999.

Kenneth Wapnick, Ph.D., *"What It Says": From the Preface of A Course in Miracles*, Foundation for *A Course in Miracles*, 2005.

Kenneth Wapnick, Ph.D., *Love Does Not Condemn: The World, the Flesh, and the Devil According to Platonism, Christianity, Gnosticism, and A Course in Miracles*, Foundation for *A Course in Miracles*, 1989.

Kenneth Wapnick, Ph.D., *Absence from Felicity: The Story of Helen Schucman and Her Scribing of A Course in Miracles*, Foundation for *A Course in Miracles*, 1991.

Nouk Sanchez and Tomas Vieira, *Take Me To Truth: Undoing the Ego*, O-Books, 2007.

Bart D. Ehrman: *Lost Christianities: The Battles for Scripture and the Faiths We Never Knew*, Oxford University Press, 2003.

Marvin Meyer, *The Gnostic Discoveries: The Impact of the Nag Hammadi Library*, HarperSanFrancisco, 2005.

James M. Robinson, Paul Hoffmann, and John S. Kloppenborg (Eds.), *The Sayings Gospel Q in Greek and English: With Parallels from the Gospels of Mark and Thomas*, Augsburg Fortress Press, 2002.

James M. Robinson, Paul Hoffmann, and John S. Kloppenborg (Eds.), *The Critical Edition of Q: A Synopsis Including the Gospels of Matthew and Luke, Mark and Thomas With English, German and French Translations of Q and Thomas (Hermeneia: Critical and Historical Commentary on the Bible)*, Augsburg Fortress Press, 2000.

Jed McKenna, *Spiritual Enlightenment: The Damnedest Thing*, Wisefool Press, 2002.

Prof. Dr. G.J. Heering, *The Fall of Christianity: A Study of Christianity, the State, and War*, New York, Fellowship Publications, 1943. The English translation, which has been long since out of print, was based on the third Dutch edition, which dated from before World War II. Meanwhile the original Dutch book was updated substantially in 1953, to account for World War II, and finally there was a posthumous fifth edition.

A note is in order. Marvin Meyer's translation of the Thomas gospel is widely regarded as authoritative, not just by Pursah in Gary's books. His account of the impact of the Nag Hammadi library in his later book, *The Gnostic Discoveries*, is also very helpful. Bart Ehrman's book *Lost Christianities* is very helpful in understanding the very wide variety of beliefs that developed in the wake of Jesus's ministry in Palestine. Unfortunately, he seems to be too much beholden to Christianity still in order to do Thomas justice, and he falls back to a defensive position and conveniently dismisses it as a fraud.[24] Elaine Pagels' work did a lot to fuel an interest in the Thomas gospel.

As far as *A Course In Miracles* is concerned, for some Gary Renard's work has served as an introduction; for others it was *A Talk Given* (listed above), by Ken Wapnick, all of whose work is highly recommended, I might add. Another more recent book by Ken Wapnick, also listed above, which may serve as an introduction to the Course, is his *"What It Says,"* in effect a commentary on the third section of the Preface to the Course.

As far as the Gospel of Mark is concerned, the work of Jan Willem Kaiser (not currently available in English) is, in my opinion, the best critical commentary, both from a linguistic and spiritual point of view, because it completely punctures the theological homogenization which plagues other translations and many commentaries. The commentary by R.T. France listed above is unique in that it does highlight the very different tone of Mark compared to the other two Synoptics (Matthew and Luke) and recognizes the mythological quality of Mark, as compared to the more historiographic qualities of the other two. Being still of Christian extraction, France misses the spiritual dimension of corruption in

---

24 While this book is being prepared for print, a new book by Ehrman, titled *God's Problem: How the Bible Fails to Answer Our Most Important Questions—Why We Suffer*, due out in the spring of 2008, is being written up already, because it seems Ehrman, who started as a fundamentalist, became successively more liberal pursuant to his studies and presently finds himself abandoning the Christian notion of God, on the grounds that a loving God would not cause so much suffering. (See article titled "Moderates Storm the Religious Battlefield," by Lisa Miller, in the December 31, 2007, issue of *Newsweek* magazine. Time will tell if—and, if so, how—that will lead to a revision of his knee-jerk Christian views on the Thomas gospel, which occasionally trips him up elsewhere in his work on early Christianity.

the transition from the Jesus teachings to the Gospels and their translations in particular, so that any comments on that aspect do go back mostly to the work of J.W. Kaiser. In due course, I hope to complete the translation of Kaiser's work into English.

Index 1 – The Logia and The Disappearance of the Universe

Note: Pursah very specifically makes the point (*Your Immortal Reality*, p. 160) that the following 22 sayings which are offered in *The Disappearance of the Universe* (DU), where they do not always appear in full, are more easily understood by a person living in our time than some of the other sayings. These 22 sayings are marked with a bold heading in the section "The Logia."

Index 2 – The Logia and the NT Gospels

Besides those Logia which Pursah identifies specifically as "prequels" to the NT literature (Logia 26, 31, 36, 54, 94, and 95; see DU pp. 79-80), there are many other instances where a connection to the NT Gospels can be seen, as noted below.

The main source for this list is the book *The Five Gospels*. In general, the reader should note that the Markan gospel has a very different quality from that of the other two Synoptics. The Markan story, besides focusing only on Jesus's ministry and not on the irrelevancies of his life in Palestine, sounds more like a myth or a fairy tale than a history, particularly when read in Greek. Translations tend to obfuscate this quality, because they have a homogenizing effect. Needless to say, it is also the oldest of the three Synoptics, dating from less than two generations after the Crucifixion, only shortly after Thomas (one generation), and its identifiable sources include Thomas and Q. Matthew and Luke are of about the same age, being dated two to three generations after the Crucifixion, and have more the character of historical novels, attempting to convince the reader that this-and-so is what really happened, except it is colored by their own sectarian interpretation. The sources for Matthew and Luke include Thomas, Q, and Mark. The Gospel of John is a bird of a different feather altogether and is dated four to five generations after the Crucifixion. Few Thomas quotes appear in it.

Note again that in these references I skip over any of the sayings which Pursah dismisses, although, from a strict standpoint of scriptural scholarship, those are equally important, but that is not our concern here. Historically, the point is that any quotations in which Thomas is clearly the source strengthen the case for the historical order in which Thomas was completed well before Paul's influence on the other gospel writers. The passages listed below are parallel passages in the biblical literature, or, if prefaced with "cf.", they are similar to the Logia, but not exact parallels. The notation closely follows the method used in *The Five Gospels*, simplified or amended to suit the needs of the present work.

- Logion 1 – "not taste death" – Jn 8:51-52.
- Logion 2 – "seek & find" – Th 92, 94; Mt 7:7-8; Lk 11:9-10; co-sourced in Q.
- Logion 3 – "within you" – cf. Th 51, 113:2-4; Lk 17:20-21.
- Logion 4 – "first and last" – Mk 10:31; Mt 20:16; Lk 13:30, 19:30; co-sourced in Q.
- Logion 5 – "hidden & revealed" – Th 6; Mk 4:22; Mt 10:26; Lk 8:17, 12:2; co-sourced in Q.
- Logion 6 – "golden rule" – Mt 7:12; Lk 6:31.
- Logion 6 – "hidden & revealed" – Th 5; Mk 4:22; Mt 10:26; Lk 8:17, 12:2.
- Logion 8 – "fisherman" – Mt 13:47-48.
- Logion 8 – "two good ears" – Th 21, 24, 65, 96; Mk 4:9.
- Logion 9 – "sower" – Mk 4:3-8; Mt 13:3-8; Lk 8:5-8a.
- Logion 11 – no NT parallels; cf. Th 111.
- Logion 13 – "Who am I?" – cf. Mk 8:27-30; Mt 16:13-20; Lk 9:18-21; Jn 1:35-42.
- Logion 14 – (NB: The second part of Logion 14 is merged as the answer to the first part of Logion 6 in P/GoTh) – "eat what is provided" – Lk 10:8; and – "what goes in" vs. "what comes out" – Mk 7:15; Mt 15:11.
- Logion 17 – "what no eye has seen" – cf. 1 Cor 2:9.
- Logion 18 – "the end" – cf. Th 1, 19.
- Logion 20 – "mustard seed" – Mk 4:30-32; Mt 13:31-32; Lk 13:18-19; co-sourced in Q.
- Logion 21 – Note that P/GoTh does not have this Logion, but parts of it widely recur in the Synoptics, further strengthening the historical relationship among these traditions.
- Logion 22 – "children in God's domain" – cf. Mk 10:13-16; Mt 18:3, 19:13; Lk 18:15-17; Jn 3:35; Th 106:1.

- Logion 61 – "things of my Father" – Mt 11:25-27; Lk 10:21-22; co-sourced in Q; cf. Jn 3:35, 13:3.
- Logion 61 – "whole and divided" – a corollary to this image is the "house divided against itself" which will not stand.
- Logion 62 – "disclosing the mysteries" – cf. Mk 4:11-12; Mt 13:11, 13-15; Lk 8:10; Jn 9:39.
- Logion 62 – "left and right hand" – Mt 6:1-4.
- Logion 63 – "rich investor" – Lk 12:16-21.
- Logion 63 – "two ears" – Th 8, 21, 24, 96; Mk 4:9.
- Logion 66 – "the rejected stone" – Mk 12:9-11; Mt 21:40-43; Lk 20:15b-18; cf. also Ps 118:22.
- Logion 72 – "disputed inheritance" – Lk 12:13-15.
- Logion 75 – "wedding chamber" – cf. Th 23, 106.
- Logion 76 – "pearl" – Mt 13:45-46.
- Logion 76 – "on possessions" – Mt 6:19-21; Lk 12:33-34; co-sourced in Q.
- Logion 79 – "lucky hearers" – Lk 11:27-28.
- Logion 80 – "world & body" – Th 56:1-2.
- Logion 86 – "foxes have dens" – Mt 8:20, Lk 9:58; co-sourced in Q.
- Logion 87 – cf. Th 112.
- Logion 89 – "inside & outside" – Mt 23:25-26; Lk 11:39-41; co-sourced in Q.
- Logion 90 – "yoke & burden" – Mt 11:28-30.
- Logion 91 – "knowing the times" – Lk 12:54-56; Mt 16:2-3; co-sourced in Q.
- Logion 92 – "seek & find" – Th 2, 94; Mt 7:7-8; Lk 11:9-10; co-sourced in Q.
- Logion 94 – "seek & knock" – Th 2, 92; Mt 7:7-8; Lk 11:9-10; co-sourced in Q.
- Logion 95 – "lend without return" – Mt 5:42b; Lk 6:34, 35c; co-sourced in Q.
- Logion 96 – "leaven" – Mt 13:33; Lk 13:20-21; co-sourced in Q.
- Logion 96 – "two ears" – Th 8:4, 21:10, 24:2, 65:8; Mk 4:9.

Index 3 – Authenticity of the Logia according to Pursah, versus the opinion of the Jesus Seminar

The listing below presents only the Logia that Pursah endorses as authentic and which are the subject of this book, cross-indexed to the opinions about the same phrases from the Scholars Version, as it can be found in the book *The Five Gospels*. The text throughout is Pursah's version. Even a casual glance reveals that the conclusions arrived at via these two paths are remarkably different. Needless to say, this list completely omits the Logia and material which Pursah dismisses; however, in varying degrees many of them are met with approval from the Jesus Seminar, which makes the distinction between these two approaches clearer yet again.

Historically, the Jesus Seminar believes that the Thomas material came together in the 70-100 CE period, but that the kernel of it predates the Synoptics. This notion of the chronology broadly coincides with Pursah's version of events, namely, that her version of seventy sayings were the original kernel and that the accretion of extra verbal ballast and corruption led to the version of 114 sayings, which we now know from the find at Nag Hammadi (NH). On page 474 of *The Five Gospels*, here is how the authors put it: "Thomas probably assumed its present form by 100 CE, although an earlier edition may have originated as early as 50-60 CE."

It behooves us to reflect at this point that the two methods under consideration are different from each other at every level. Pursah speaks with the authority of personal acquaintance in her identity as the former apostle Thomas, and, if you accept that, as this book does, then this is conclusive. The text-critical method of the Jesus Seminar—and of any serious scholar in the usual academic sense—simply follows a different set of rules from those used here. The reader should therefore not conclude that there is anything wrong with textual scholarship in general or the methods of the Jesus Seminar in particular. These scholars are preeminent in their field, and their scholarship is unquestionably some of the best the world has to offer, but inevitably their method goes by form (especially historical order), not content. And so, by following a different set of rules, the conclusions we reach are markedly different of necessity.

A small example will suffice to clarify this point and will be self-evident to anyone studying the Course. The learning process of the Course proceeds from familiarity with the book to application of its principles, which then leads to greater depth of understanding; many of us marvel time and again that it is taking us deeper and deeper and deeper. The strength of this experience will grow over time to the point where we can heed what Jesus suggests in the Course: "Forget this world, forget this course, and come with wholly empty hands unto your God." (ACIM:W-189.7:5) In short, the Course points us in a direction towards an experience, but in due time, experience will be with us, and the book becomes so much dead weight, printed matter. Along those lines, if a textual scholar saw two versions of a text which he could date with certainty as fifty years apart, and there was a fragment of a sentence in the second but not in the first, the tendency would be to think it was added (later) to the second, rather than omitted from the first. The person who had the inner experience in their own relationship with Jesus might be able to recognize without any doubt or hesitation that the second variant were the original and the older text had an omission, not the other way around. But since there are no objective criteria for validating such experience by outsiders, we remain on our own in this case, and it is up to each one of us to discriminate for ourselves.

In reflecting on these differences of opinion carefully, the pattern that seems to suggest itself is that many of the sayings which Pursah retains as undoubtedly authentic are more than likely suspected of "gnosticising" tendencies by the Jesus Seminar. And so, barring specific textual evidence, the mental model may still be one of treating Jesus as a proto-Christian in the orthodox mold when attempting to sort out the authentic material from the later additions, and, accordingly, Pursah and the Jesus Seminar are frequently at odds in this area. After you reflect on it for a while, the differences are really hilarious, and there is no wonder that Jesus in the Course goes to some lengths to clarify that he is not the "bitter idols" that have been made of him. (ACIM:C-5.5:7)

A statistical summary of the results in the following table is revealing: clearly, the opinion of the Jesus Seminar on the sayings which Pursah retains is almost (in round numbers) 45% No, 24% Maybe, 26% Probably, and 5% Yes. It gets more interesting if you realize that in the resounding "Yes" cases, there is 100% agreement between the two. By and large, the issue would seem to be that the Jesus Seminar is looking for a Jesus who is a proto-Christian, and that expectation does not coincide with the vantage point of Pursah and the Course.

Notes about the table:

1. The Jesus Seminar uses a very handy color-coding system in *The Five Gospels*, but here I shall follow a verbal description: their red becomes "yes" (75-100% probable authenticity); pink becomes "probably" (50-75% probable authenticity); grey "doubtful" (25-50% probable authenticity); and black "no" (0-25% probable authenticity).

2. Please also note that the conclusions of the Jesus Seminar address only the authenticity of the actual Jesus quotes themselves and none of the surrounding text. The column heading is "5G", indicating the book *The Five Gospels*. Some sections are broken down to phrases, or even sub-sentences, to accommodate different ratings by the Jesus Seminar. Interestingly in some cases, sections they reject coincide with rejections by Pursah.

Logion	Text - Pursah's Gospel of Thomas	5G
1	Whosoever discovers the interpretation of these sayings will not taste death.	No
2	Those who seek should not stop seeking until they find. When they find, they will be disturbed.	Probably
	When they are disturbed, they will marvel, and they will reign over all.	No
3	If your teachers say to you, 'Look, God's Divine Rule is in the sky,' then the birds will precede you. If they say to you, 'It's in the sea,' then the fish will precede you. Rather, God's Divine Rule is within you and you are everywhere.	Doubtful
	When you know yourself, you will be known, and you will understand that we are one. But if you don't know yourself, you live in poverty, and you are the poverty.	No
4	The person old in days should not hesitate to ask a little child the meaning of life, and that person will live.	No
	For many of the first will be last,	Doubtful
	And they will become a single one.	No
5	Know what is in front of your face, and what is hidden from you will be disclosed to you.	Doubtful
	For there is nothing hidden that will not be revealed.	Maybe
6 (14)	When you go into any region and walk in the countryside, and people take you in, eat what they serve you.	Maybe

	After all, what goes into your mouth will not defile you; rather, it's what comes out of your mouth that will reveal you.	Maybe
8	A wise fisherman cast his net into the sea. When he drew it up it was full of little fish. Among them he discovered a large, fine fish. He threw all the little fish back into the sea, and he chose the large fish.	No
	Anyone here with two good ears should listen.	Doubtful
9	Look, the sower went out, took a handful of seeds, and scattered them. Some fell on the road, and the birds came and ate them. Others fell on the rocks, and they didn't take root and didn't produce grain. Others fell on the thorns, and they choked the seed and the worms ate them. And others fell on good soil, and it produced a good crop; it yielded sixty per measure and one hundred twenty per measure.	Maybe
11	The dead are not alive, and the living will not die.	Yes [25]
13	Compare me to something and tell me what I am like.	No
	NB: The NH version has another Jesus quote, which the Jesus Seminar rates 'No,' and which Pursah omits from her version, but she retains the narrative.	
17	I will give you what no eye has seen, what no ear has heard, what no hand has touched, and what has not arisen in the human heart.	No
18	Have you discovered the beginning, then, so that you are seeking the end? For where the beginning is, the end will be. Fortunate is the one who stands at the beginning: That one will know the end	No

263

---

25 The NH version is much longer, and for the most part rated 'No' by the Jesus Seminar, but Pursah retains this one statement as authentic.

and will not taste death.

20	It's like a mustard seed. It's the smallest of all seeds, but when it falls on prepared soil, it produces a large plant and becomes a shelter for the birds of the sky.	Yes
22	When you make the two into one, and when you make the inner like the outer and the outer like the inner, and the upper like the lower, and when you make male and female into a single one, so the male will not be male and the female will not be female…then you will enter the Kingdom.	No
23	I shall choose you, one from a thousand and two from ten thousand, and they shall stand as a single one.	No
24	Anyone here with two ears had better listen! There is a light within a person of light, and it shines on the whole world. If it does not shine, it is dark.	No
26	You see the speck that is in your brother's eye, but you do not see the log that is in your own eye. When you take the log out of your own eye, then you will see clearly enough to take the speck out of your brother's eye.	Probably
28	I stood in the world and found them all drunk, and I did not find any of them thirsty. They came into the world empty, and they seek to leave the world empty. But meanwhile they are drunk. When they shake off their wine, they will open their eyes.	No
31	A prophet is not acceptable in his home town.	Probably
	A doctor does not heal those who know him.	Maybe
32	A city built on a high hill and fortified cannot fall, nor can it be hidden.	Probably

34	If a blind person leads a blind person, both of them will fall into a hole.	Maybe
36	Do not worry, from morning to night and from night until morning, about what you will wear. The lilies neither toil nor spin.	Probably
37	When you take your clothes off without guilt, and you put them under your feet like little children and trample them, then you will see the son of the living one and will not be afraid.	No
40	A grapevine has been planted outside of the Father, but since it is not strong, it will be pulled up by its roots and shall pass away.	Maybe
41	Whoever has something in hand will be given more, and whoever has nothing will be deprived of even the little they have.	Probably
42	Be passersby.	Maybe
45	Grapes are not harvested from thorn trees, nor are figs gathered from thistles.[26]	Probably
47	A person cannot mount two horses or bend two bows.	No
	And a servant cannot serve two masters, or that servant will honor the one and offend the other. Nobody drinks aged wine and immediately wants to drink young wine. Young wine is not poured into old wineskins, or they might break, and aged wine is not poured into new wineskins, or it might spoil.	Probably
	An old patch is not sewn onto a new garment, since it would create a tear.	Maybe

26 Pursah omits two thirds compared to the NH version, which JS rates "maybe" and "no."

48	If two make peace with each other in a single house, they will say to the mountain, 'Move over here!' and it will move.	Maybe
49	Fortunate are those who are alone and chosen, for you will find the Kingdom. For you have come from it, and you will return there again.	No
51	What you are looking forward to has come, but you don't know it.	No
52	You have disregarded the living one who is in your presence, and have spoken of the dead.	No
54	Fortunate are the poor, for yours is the Father's Kingdom.	Yes
56	Whoever has come to understand this world has found merely a corpse, and whoever has discovered the corpse, of that one the world is no longer worthy.	No
57	God's Divine Rule is like a person who had good seed. His rival came during the night and sowed weeds among the good seed. The person did not let the workers pull up the weeds, but said to them, 'No, otherwise you might pull up the weeds and pull up the wheat along with them. For on the day of the harvest the weeds will be conspicuous, and will be pulled up and burned.'	Maybe
58	Congratulations to the person who has forgiven and has found life.	No
59	Look to the living One as long as you live. Otherwise, when you die and then try to see the living One, you will be unable to see.	No
61	I am the one who comes from what is whole. I was given from the things of my Father. Therefore, I say that if one is whole, one will be filled with light, but if one is divided, one will be filled with darkness.	No

62	I disclose my mysteries to those who are ready for my mysteries.	No
	Do not let your left hand know what your right hand is doing.	Probably
63	There was a rich person who had a great deal of money. He said: 'I shall invest my money so that I may sow, reap, plant, and fill my storehouses with produce, that I may lack nothing.' These were the things he was thinking in his heart, but that very night he died.	Probably
66	Show me the stone that the builders rejected. That is the keystone.	No
67	Those who know all, but are lacking in themselves, are completely lacking.	No
70	If you bring forth what is within you, what you have will save you. If you do not have that within you, what you do not have within you will kill you.	No
72	Brother, who made me a divider?	Maybe
	I'm not a divider, am I?	Maybe
75	There are many standing at the door, but those who are alone will enter the bridal suite.	No
76	God's Divine Rule is like a merchant who had a supply of merchandise and then found a pearl. That merchant was prudent; he sold the merchandise and bought the single pearl for himself.	Probably
	So also with you, seek the treasure that is unfailing, that is enduring, where no moth comes to eat and no worm destroys.	Maybe
79	Lucky are those who have heard the word of the Father and have truly kept it. For there will be	Maybe

	days when you will say: 'Lucky are the womb that has not conceived and the breasts that have not given milk.'	
80	Whoever has come to know the world has discovered the body, and whoever has discovered the body, of that one the world is not worthy.	No
85	Adam came from great power and great wealth, but he was not worthy of you. For had he been worthy, he would not have tasted death.	No
86	Foxes have their dens and birds have their nests, but human beings have no place to lay down and rest.	Probably
87	How miserable is the body that depends on a body, and how miserable is the soul that depends on these two.	No
88	The messengers and the prophets will come to you and give you what belongs to you. You, in turn, give them what you have, and say to yourselves, 'When will they come and take what belongs to them?'	No
89	Why do you wash the outside of the cup? Don't you understand that the one who made the inside is also the one who made the outside?	Probably
90	Come to me, for my yoke is comfortable and my lordship is gentle, and you will find rest for yourselves.	No
91	You examine the face of Heaven and earth, but you have not come to know the one who is in your presence, and you do not know how to examine the present moment.	Maybe

92	Seek and you will find.	Probably
	In the past, however, I did not tell you the things about which you asked me then. Now I am willing to tell them, but you are not seeking them.	No
94	One who seeks will find. And for one who knocks, it shall be opened.	Probably
95	If you have money, do not lend it at interest. Rather, give it to someone who will not pay you back.	Probably
96	God's Divine Rule is like a woman. She took a little leaven, hid it in dough, and made it into large loaves of bread.	Probably
	Anyone here with two ears had better listen!	Maybe
97	God's Divine Rule is like a woman who was carrying a jar full of meal. While she was walking along a distant road, the handle of the jar broke, and the meal spilled behind her along the road. She didn't know it; she hadn't noticed a problem. When she reached her house, she put the jar down and discovered it was empty.	Probably
99	Those here who do what my Father wants are my brothers and my mother.	Probably
	They are the ones who will enter the Father's Kingdom.	Maybe
100	Give the Emperor what belongs to the Emperor. Give God what belongs to God.	Yes
103	Congratulations to those who know where the rebels are going to attack. They can get going, collect their Divine resources, and be prepared before the rebels arrive.	Maybe

#		
106	When you make the two into one, you will become children of Adam,	No
	and when you say, 'Mountain move from here!' it will move.	Maybe
107	God's Divine Rule is like a shepherd who had a hundred sheep. One of them, the largest, went astray. He left the ninety-nine and looked for the one until he found it. After he had toiled, he said to the sheep, 'I love you more than the ninety-nine.'	Maybe
108	Whoever drinks from my mouth shall become like me. I myself shall become that person and the hidden things will be revealed to that person.	No
109	God's Divine Rule is like a person who had a treasure hidden in his field but did not know it. And when he died he left it to his son. The son did not know about it either. He took over the field and sold it. The buyer went plowing, discovered the treasure, and began to lend money at interest to whomever he wished.	Probably
110	Let one who has found the world, and has become wealthy, renounce the world.	No
111	The Heavens and the earth will roll up in your presence, and whoever is living with the living one will not see death. Did I not say, 'Those who have found themselves, of them the world is not worthy'?	No
113	It will not come by watching for it. It will not be said, 'Behold here,' or 'Behold there.' Rather, the Kingdom of the Father is spread out upon the earth, and people do not see it.	Probably

Cover Art: Teach Only Love

The painting on the cover of this book is by Samuel Augustin of Brooklyn, New York. Sam has been a friend of Rogier's for many years. He has come to the Course from a Seventh Day Adventist background, which is the center of his social life in a Haitian community in Brooklyn. He has been studying *A Course in Miracles* intermittently for many years, and after the French edition of the Course appeared in 2006, Rogier and Sam started a French study group on the Course, which initially met in Sam's studio. To see some of Sam's work, go to: www.kreyolart.com

The painting is an expression of Sam's personal journey with the Course and, in particular, his growing understanding that the Jesus of the Course speaks to us, not as the suffering savior of Christianity, but as the presence of unconditional Love in our lives, which is available to us at any time we choose to let him in. In the dialog at the time Sam was still working on the painting, Rogier asked him, "Couldn't Jesus be coming through the window?" A few brush strokes...*et voilá!* This rendition depicts the Jesus of the Course, as well as in the Thomas Logia, as a Jesus who is speaking direct to you, the reader. So instead of an idol we hang on the wall, he comes to life for us and is available to us as a guide on our journey, if only we ask him in. Of course, he addresses us as mind, that is, he calls us to awaken from the identification with our dream-role and to know we have another choice, which is to follow him to his Kingdom *not* of this world. Everything depends on inviting him in as our Internal Teacher, as the Course calls it, and accepting that relationship into our lives. For without that guidance, at best we will have another storybook—a fairy tale— for children. If we do, however, allow ourselves to feel his presence and hear his message, he will come walking right off the page and be present for us.

Also, the overriding emphasis of the painting is on the presence of love, which flows to us through Jesus (specific features are blurred). This can be seen not only in the context of docetic traditions like the Acts of John, but also in the context of Helen's dream experience, in which, quite to her amazement, she realized that Jesus looked just like Bill, as reported by Ken Wapnick in his book *Absence from Felicity*. (See Bibliography.)

The painting thus became a collaborative project, and Rogier chose the words "Teach Only Love" as the title, based on the section in the Course where Jesus explains the true message of the crucifixion:

> That is why you must teach only one lesson. If you are to be conflict-free yourself, you must learn only from the Holy Spirit and teach only by Him. You are only love, but when you deny this, you make what you are something you must learn to remember. I said before that the message of the crucifixion was, "Teach only love, for that is what you are." This is the one lesson that is perfectly unified, because it is the only lesson that is one. Only by teaching it can you learn it. "As you teach so will you learn." If that is true, and it is true indeed, do not forget that what you teach is teaching you. And what you project or extend you believe. (ACIM:T-6.III.2)

Reprints of the painting are available as part of a fund-raising program for this teaching initiative and related activities, which are organized under a not-for-profit organization. Information can be found at:

http://www.thecourseintongues.org/Teach_Only_Love.html

BOOKS

O books
O is a symbol of the world, of oneness and unity. In
different cultures it also means the "eye", symbolizing
knowledge and insight, and in Old English it means "place
of love or home". O books explores the many paths of
understanding which different traditions have developed
down the ages, particularly those today that express
respect for the planet and all of life.

For more information on the full list of over 300 titles
please visit our website
www.O-books.net

NOTES

NOTES

" what you deny you project 29
Quan Yin 30
Holy Spirit 36

NOTES

NOTES

NOTES

NOTES

NOTES